# Creating Spaces of Wellbeing and Belonging for Refugee and Asylum-Seeker Students

This practical resource for principals and school leaders provides guidance on how to develop schools into places of belonging for all children, especially children of refugee and asylum-seeker backgrounds. It demonstrates the need for school leaders to be informed, reflective individuals and highlights the role that leaders can play in a school culture that provides a safe place and effective educational opportunities for these students. Written in an accessible manner, each chapter includes a summary of theory and vignettes from school leaders that outline approaches, challenges, critical reflections and suggestions for how their experiences can be adapted to other contexts. Principals' voices and experiences from across the globe are included, representing a range of school levels including primary and secondary, large and small enrolments, religious and public, and urban and rural settings.

This book is intended for use in schools by school principals and aspiring school leaders, and by educational professionals engaged in supporting schools with students with refugee backgrounds.

**Scott Imig** is Deputy Head of the School of Education and directs the leadership program at the University of Newcastle, Australia. His research is primarily focused on the preparation and support of school leaders and teachers to meet the needs of all students.

**Maura Sellars** is a Doctor of Philosophy and is currently a lecturer at the University of Newcastle, NSW, Australia after spending 30 years as a teacher, curriculum leader and school leader in primary schools. As an inclusivist, her most recent research has focused on the authentic integration of students with refugee and asylum-seeker experiences into Western classrooms.

**John Fischetti** is Pro Vice-Chancellor of the College of Human and Social Futures at the University of Newcastle, Australia. His primary focus is on school transformation and rethinking learning and teaching.

# Creating Spaces of Wellbeing and Belonging for Refugee and Asylum-Seeker Students

Skills and Strategies for School Leaders

Scott Imig, Maura Sellars and John Fischetti

Routledge
Taylor & Francis Group

LONDON AND NEW YORK

First published 2022
by Routledge
2 Park Square, Milton Park, Abingdon, Oxon OX14 4RN

and by Routledge
605 Third Avenue, New York, NY 10158

*Routledge is an imprint of the Taylor & Francis Group, an informa business*

*British Library Cataloguing-in-Publication Data*
A catalogue record for this book is available from the British Library

*Library of Congress Cataloging-in-Publication Data*
Names: Sellars, Maura, author. | Imig, Scott, author. | Fischetti, John, author.
Title: Creating spaces of wellbeing and belonging for refugee and asylum seeker students : skills and strategies for school leaders / Maura Sellars, Scott Imig and John Fischetti.
Identifiers: LCCN 2021004399 | ISBN 9780367548209 (hardback) | ISBN 9780367548230 (paperback) | ISBN 9781003090731 (ebook)
Subjects: LCSH: Refugee children--Education. | Refugee children--Psychology. | Belonging (Social psychology) in children. | School principals--Anecdotes. | School environment. | Multicultural education. | Educational leadership. | Reflective learning.
Classification: LCC LC3719 .S45 2021 | DDC 370.86/914--dc23
LC record available at https://lccn.loc.gov/2021004399

ISBN: 978-0-367-54820-9 (hbk)
ISBN: 978-0-367-54823-0 (pbk)
ISBN: 978-1-003-09073-1 (ebk)

DOI: 10.4324/9781003090731

Typeset in Bembo
by Taylor & Francis Books

# Contents

# Acknowledgements

Thank you to the talented principals from around the world who gave of their time to participate in this research. Your professionalism and insights into leading schools attempting to authentically integrate children and families with refugee and asylum-seeker experiences are invaluable. Thanks to Kathleen Smithers for immersing yourself in this research and for offering wonderful suggestions along the way. Thanks to Dr. Sally Patfield for your keen insights and support. Thanks also to Dr. Tra Do for your skill, care and effort in supporting this work.

# Introduction

As we write this, the world is in a state of upheaval. Nearly 70 million human beings have been forcibly displaced from their homes due to war and conflict and of these individuals, 28 million are classified as refugees or asylum seekers. Many of these men, women and children who have experienced unimaginable loss and trauma, find themselves living in new countries, with a new language, new cultures, radically different expectations and new forms of schooling.

We are academics and teachers in a school of education at a regional Australian university and have developed strong and mutually beneficial relationships with principals who lead our local schools. Over the past few years, these leaders have increasingly voiced concern about their ability to meet the enormous challenge of supporting and educating newly arrived Middle Eastern and North African children and families with refugee and asylum-seeker experiences. The placement of these students in a regional area dominated by an almost exclusively white, Eurocentric population brought unforeseen challenges and encounters in their school communities in addition to adding richness and diversity to school populations. To ensure that they were able to plan pathways for success for these students as part of their student body, these principals were seeking research-based and practice-informed ideas about how to develop schools to effectively address acculturation, trauma, racism, pedagogy, community and wellbeing. Their calls for support, and the lack of available resources developed for and with principals, were the spark for our work.

In researching this book, we engaged with our global networks to identify and interview exceptional school leaders in five countries (Australia, England, New Zealand, Northern Ireland, and the United States of America), who are working hard every day to support children and families with refugee experiences. Our participants represent a range of schools including primary and secondary, large and small enrolments, religious and government, and urban and rural settings. These principals alerted us to the challenges and difficulties they had experienced, and indeed, were still experiencing, in addition to detailing their contexts and sharing with us their successes, perspectives, strategies and approaches to inclusion. In the chapters that follow, research literature is presented along with practical anecdotes and insights from our participating principals. We then reflect on the shared stories and relate them to the theory discussed. These lessons from our participating principals as they have applied them in their diverse contexts provide opportunities for other school leaders in a variety of school communities to reflect on the experiences of others and perhaps customise some of the strategies to further support their own communities. It is our hope that the lessons and insights shared in this book will encourage and assist principals around the world to create places of safety and belonging for their newly arrived children and families, offering both education and empathy.

# 1 The reflective leader

## Introduction

School leadership is a demanding, unpredictable and, at times, highly stressful career. Due to the pressures of the role, time-poor principals tend to operate on the fly, in a reactive posture as they interact with students, parents, staff and community members. This approach is not ideal when making practical and policy decisions with real-life implications for individual children and families. For principals who find themselves serving children and families with refugee and asylum-seeker backgrounds, who bring experiences of trauma and vast cultural differences, the challenge of thoughtful decision-making is further amplified. This chapter positions the imperative of reflection as a tool for effective decision-making; it presents conceptions of reflection and reflective processes in the research literature and offers unique perspectives on reflection from school leaders around the world.

## Why reflection?

Reflection has been the focus of much academic writing. It is difficult to determine the single most appropriate definition, but the authors agree that it is the deliberate, purposeful, metacognitive activity in which professionals engage to improve their professional practice. Reflexivity is the term used to reflect deliberately on an individual's own responses or actions in any educational context. Among all the models of reflection that have been developed to support informed educational practices, there are four common elements. Firstly, principals need to identify and consider the situations, circumstances or incidents that have prompted reflection. Secondly, in undertaking the reflective process itself, what needs to be determined is the type of reflection required, the diverse opinions around the reflection and the opinions about the reflective process selected. Thirdly, the actual content of the reflection needs to be extrapolated, determining what it is that needs to be analysed, to be discussed or challenged and what are the epistemologies and ideologies that underpin these circumstances, situations or actions. Finally, what may be the result of the reflection? What improved understanding of this aspect of professional practice has occurred as the result of the reflection? (Sellars, 2017, pp. 2–3).

DOI: 10.4324/9781003090731-1

Dewey considered reflection an essential cognitive process in which all teachers and their leaders needed to engage. He writes of reflection as: 'The active, persistent and careful consideration of any belief or supposed form of knowledge in the light of the grounds that support it and the further conclusions to which it tends' (Dewey, 1933, p. 9).

He considered reflection to be based on thinking in a particular manner; logical, rational analysis of the problem and the attention paid to the way in which these thoughts are ordered and connected meaningfully. He then envisaged that this chain of thought be analysed for assumptions, value judgements and underlying beliefs that had influenced the thinking and which in turn required investigating for evidence to support them. This was presented as a scientific method of evaluating good practice, professional decision-making and undertaking the reflective process. This was Dewey's approach as he sought to distinguish reflective thinking from everyday arbitrary thinking and, most especially, from impulsive thinking and actions. Calderhead (1989, p. 44) noted this Deweyan approach of rationally and scientifically examining issues and all their components before determining the most appropriate action to take as resulting in what Dewey himself called 'intelligent action'. In the process, the professional must undergo some uncertainty and doubt before finally determining a rational action or approach to take to the issue in question. The discomfort caused by this uncertainty became the catalyst for Boyd and Fales' (1983) six-step process of reflective practice designed to focus on learning from experience.

Proposing that learning from experience or experimental learning is not predominantly outcome based but rather that the learning is in the process, Boyd and Fales (1983) contend that it is in the participation in reflective practice that perceptions and frames of references are challenged and changed, not in the resultant action taken, thus confirming that the difference between an individual who repeats the same mistakes and one who is changed, affectively and cognitively, is their engagement in the reflective process. Quoting one of their research participants who was asked to reflect on the process of reflection itself and trying to explain what she understood to be its non-linear nature, they note that she expressed this well:

> Reflecting back inside what that has meant to you, externalising it, and internalising it, I think that's part of what reflection would be. The very word reflect has to have something there *from* which you're coming *to* something and maybe back again – a kind of spiral – or back and forth, back and forth.
>
> (Boyd & Fales, 1983, pp. 105–106; italics in the original)

The six-step model that these authors developed was based on the responses from their participants. They understand the reflective process as:

1    A feeling of discomfort;
2    Identification or clarification of the concern;

3    Openness to new information from internal or external sources, with the ability to observe and take in from a variety of perspectives;
4    Resolution, expressed as 'integration', 'coming together', 'acceptance of self-reality' and 'creative synthesis';
5    Establishing continuity of self with past present and future;
6    Deciding on whether to act on the outcome of the reflective process.
(Boyd & Fales, 1983, p. 106)

This basic model, although conceived some decades ago, provides a step-by-step process with which principals are invited to consider the challenges in the following chapters. It provides an opportunity to reflect on the comments of peers who have participated in the research, in conjunction with the theoretical underpinning, to present and guide other perspectives and to inform on each of the key topics that emerged from this initial research. It also provides a chance to engage with the critical reflection of others who seek to understand and to share knowledge and strategies, incidents and experiences that provide the data for this writing and, hopefully, encourage each of you to reflect as leaders of educational communities who support students with refugee and asylum experiences.

### Research findings

Nearly every principal we interviewed in our research talked about the need for continuous reflection when faced with the challenge of serving children and families with refugee and asylum-seeker backgrounds. Two individuals who offered keen insights were a high school principal in Australia and a high school leader in New Zealand.

> Context: My school's student population is 1,400, with students in Grades 9–13. I've been in my role now for about 16 years. I've seen students come through, and now they have siblings who are coming through the school and there are former refugee students, families and siblings, too.

> *We've got this Congolese support worker. We were paying her to work but she wasn't coming to school on any regular basis. She had been employed 15 hours a week, she was there the whole year and I had no idea where she was spending her hours. I was saying to one of my other colleagues, "I'm going to get her to fill in a timesheet, so I can catch up on everything she's doing", I was looking at it very much from an Anglo-Saxon, white perspective. And then, slowly as time went on, I've got to know the worker and sat in the conversations listening to her. I realised she's so valuable. She doesn't work in the way that we do, in terms of coming to work and being somewhere. Her work, it is all relational, and within the community. As a leader, for me, it involves learning how to work with people in the community, in terms of employing staff.*

Context: My school is a high school (Grades 7–12), with around 430 students. We have an Intensive English Centre for newly arrived students. I have been principal here for over 20 years. My career trajectory has been sort of mainstream, but with multicultural and English as a Second Language perspectives, and human rights specific perspectives becoming more important in that.

*I went into a hostile environment at the school. It was hostile and it had entrenched racism. It was hostile to a lot of the kids. There was a casual dismissal of children, which was entrenched in the school's culture. I had a huge cultural battle to fight in the school. But you don't do it by walking in and saying, "all right, everything's changed overnight." During the time of change, I sat through some gruesomely painful executive meetings. First, I listened to people. This means listening to the ladies in the office and they told me a great deal about the school, things that other people might have not wanted me to know. I listened to the young teachers who told me "we don't have anyone to talk to in school, they're all old" – which informed the way that I asked for replacement staff. If you ever wanted a definition of a stuck school, this school was that. I introduced the idea of a consensus, that decision-making didn't have to be top down, that people could contribute to it. If you contributed, then you have a say in it. If you stood aside from contributing, you really didn't have any right to have a say. I flattened all the hierarchies; and of course, this all got me undying hatred from a couple of the chaps.*

### Unique contexts, global principles

Though separated by the Tasman Sea and a wealth of cultural differences, these two principals share an understanding of the importance of reflection and seeking new understandings when faced with uncomfortable situations. The high school leader from New Zealand has a long history of working to understand and support her diverse families, yet when exposed to the non-western work practices of her Congolese staff member, she felt compelled to reflect on her discomfort and seek more information. The Australian principal found herself thrust into a far more difficult environment that operated in a hierarchical and callous manner that challenged her integrity. Though naturally assertive, as a new leader, she tempered herself and gathered information from office staff and young teachers, individuals who are often not consulted in school decision-making. This information source both provided her with a unique vantage point and helped develop a collaborative structure in her school. Both leaders recognised a discomfort in themselves and spent time working to understand what was causing their discomfort. The way these two leaders operate, the way they purposefully seek new knowledge and understandings before responding to unique challenges, helps them to create positive school environments for their staff, students and families.

School leaders are faced with hundreds of decisions daily. While experience can offer much guidance for seemingly routine decision-making, principals must remain attuned to the sense of personal discomfort certain challenges elicit. Discomfort stems from uncertainty and it is a trigger for reflective practice. Developing a process for reflection is necessary for school leaders and the six-steps outlined by Boyd and Fales (1983) can be very supportive. Their reflection process enables school leaders to address their discomfort by purposefully focusing on it to ascertain why it is concerning and determine what information they need. This reflection process allows them to determine what action, if any, is necessary. To amplify the power of this approach, leaders can train their entire staff to engage in the six-step process. Creating a culture that employs such a process is vital for dealing with difference and integration and continuously reflecting on what is best for all students, including those with refugee and asylum-seeker experiences.

## Critical reflection

Despite the importance of Dewey's thinking around reflection, critics have responded that it may be just that, thinking about the incidences, situations or occurrences without any emphasis on action. For some, this left a component missing from the reflective cycle, which was, for them, the purpose and the product of the process of reflection itself (Gore & Zeichner, 1991; Noffke & Brennan, 1988). Calderhead (1989) has been dismissive of any reflection that does not complete the cycle and include action. While there are many situations in which principals can take action as a result of their reflective practice, it is not always simple or even possible to achieve. This is most apparent when working with critical reflection that engages with social reconstructionist themes or issues which involve social or political aspects of schooling. When engaging with the reflective process as an everyday practice for principals, it becomes apparent that there are different levels of reflective thinking, some simple, some more complex, and the actions that can be affected as the products of these diverse incidents or situations are correspondingly simple or complex (Gore, 1987, p. 121). Gore and Zeichner (1991) developed a taxonomic model of the levels of thinking in which practitioners may engage. It comprises four levels, each more complex in purpose, process and potential product:

1    An academic version, which focuses on teachers' skills in disseminating discipline content and presenting it in such a way as to maximise its accessibility for students;
2    A social efficacy model version, which is based on research findings and focuses on evidence-based practice;
3    A developmental version, which primarily considers age and developmentally appropriate teaching strategies that focus on students' interests and thinking;
4    A social reconstructionist version, in which reflection is focused on the political and social issues of schooling and on classroom interactions designed to promote greater student equity and justice.

While each of these 'versions' have their place in the professional thinking that principals must necessarily engage with as part of their professional work, much of the purpose and the resultant products for principals who are supporting the emotional, social and academic development of students with refugee and asylum-seeker experiences must be focused on the social efficacy, developmental and social reconstructionist types of reflection.

These 'versions' of reflection are often complicated by the strictures of systemic rules, regulations, mandatory curricula and reporting and the school procedures and policies. Complications arise when the interpolation of these three versions of reflection involve reflective thinking about *how* the research-based evidence can be effectively customised into practice which is appropriate for individual principals' own teaching context and school climate. The conflicts and challenges of providing age-related developmentally appropriate programs of learning and experiences for students who are not only traumatised but may have abnormal developmental trajectories with regard to brain maturation is one that many principals must face. This is not only in the context of providing for students who have traumatic childhood and adolescent experiences or intergenerational trauma, but, in the case of students with refugee and asylum-seeker backgrounds, those who may also have interrupted schooling, very little educational opportunity or no school experiences at all despite their ages. The additional impact of school cultures, subcultures, institutional and systemic racism may prove to be a considerable hindrance to principals who attempt to change the ways in which other members of the school community respond to, and interact with, newcomers who have multiple degrees of difference from the majority culture.

While this taxonomy of critical reflection does not necessarily make the process of complex reflection easier for principals who attempt to integrate students with refugee and asylum experiences into their communities, it may help clarify the purpose of the reflection, most especially if the situation that is the identified source of unease is the complex interpolation of all three varieties of the model. It may facilitate a step-by-step approach to planning and providing short-term effective goals for integration as the products of the reflection. From these first actions, transparency of purpose is possible as longer-term actions can be identified as the consequence of more complex reflective thinking and reflexive interrogation into these initial actions. The critical factor in all levels of reflection, critical or otherwise, is the capacity of principals to engage in the reflective process with clear purpose and informed actions which are customised to their unique context and community. Each principal must conscientiously consider their own beliefs and values, their commitment to supporting each student in their school and the ways in which they can effectively and sensitively engage with the multiple roles with which they are entrusted (Leithwood et al., 2017).

## Research findings

Two leaders who offered keen insights about the need for critical reflection were a primary principal in Northern Ireland and a high school principal in the United States.

Context: At the moment, we would have probably two out of every six children that would be asylum seeker or possibly going for citizenship at the moment. In total we have around 80% newcomer students.

*I've sent a number of what I might call my more resistant staff on some courses because I feel the most important thing is to understand that the children have so many needs to fulfil before we can teach them. They must understand that the children need to be cared for, before they are able to learn anything. So, my main thing, at the moment, is now to change our school policies to reflect that. That's why we've recently changed our Positive Behaviour Policy to a Positive Relationships Policy. We still need to do quite a lot of learning. I maintain that the day that I think I know everything is also the day that I should retire! I still have a couple of staff who insist that, "He needs to be punished. She needs to go to detention," for minor misdemeanours. That, we know from research, has been a practice that just doesn't work. For the sake of all our children, not just the refugees and asylum seekers, we must persuade our staff that a nurturing approach is something that we really need to adopt, right across the school.*

Context: This is my 19th year in education. I've been in administration for about the last seven or eight; I've worked at three different schools as an administrator. My previous school was more urban and lower socio-economic than my current school, but both have received newcomers and refugee students.

*I just received my doctorate in educational leadership a couple weeks back. In my school, we had quite a few refugee students, I was so impressed by them. Then it became I was so disappointed by how I felt we were serving them, and how I saw the delivery of our services. And so those two things really pushed kind of where I'm at. I think very early on, it was clear that was going to be the area I pursued for my dissertation. In my classroom teaching days, even then, there was this sense of, this is isn't good, this isn't – I'm not helping this young man that was in my class at that time. That is the frustration with some of the things that are imposed upon us. Sometimes they are not educationally sound, or what educational research would say what we need to be doing, but are politically driven and pushed in. And so now trying to kind of merge those things, I mean, I understand that they are going to be things we have to do from a political standpoint; but to try to do those in an educationally sound way is the big thing. After everything I have seen, I think we need to come up with a better way to support and serve these young people in a way that is helpful for them and allows them also to achieve the kind of goal post that education has put in front of them.*

*Unique contexts, global principles*

Despite living in different countries, leading different-level schools and serving massively different numbers of students with refugee and asylum-seeker backgrounds, each of our principals spoke of the challenges of working within a system that doesn't always work in the best interests of all students. The primary principal from Northern Ireland recognises a need for reshaping school policies and re-educating her staff to accept and respond to student differences. A nurturing leader, she understands that many of her staff members comfortably operate within punitive rules and punishments and she is working mightily to undo these default behaviours. The secondary leader from the United States has wrestled with the question of how to preserve his own integrity while working within a system that he thinks doesn't support his students with refugee and asylum-seeker backgrounds nor allow him to be the leader he desires to be. A passionate learner, his reflection has pushed him to earn a doctoral degree to better understand how to merge system expectations and educationally sound practices for every child. Each of our leaders reflected on social and political issues within their own schools and each made what efforts they believed they could to ameliorate those issues.

The process of reflection often emanates from a feeling of discomfort but, from there, there are many ways in which leaders can proceed. Gore and Zeichner (1991) offer four categories for reflection and challenge leaders to determine if they are reflecting on academic or developmental issues, pedagogical concerns, political or social constraints. As our leaders illustrate, school and system policies can be perceived as tying the hands of principals and shaping the parameters of academic and social support for students. School leaders who can work within policies, bump up against policies and work to revise policies operate at the top of their field. School cultures in which students with refugee and asylum-seeker backgrounds are well served spring from reflective leaders who can identify and push back against the real and perceived constraints of their roles. Moreover, leaders who empower and train their executive teams to navigate policies for the benefit of their students can exponentially expand their impact.

## Personal Reflection Model

Principals have many decisions to make as part of their professional responsibilities, many of which require them to engage in the reflective process. While the six-step model discussed earlier is an ideal model for those who are unaccustomed to the process, as reflection becomes more habitual, it can be useful to engage with a Personal Reflection Model, which facilitates an explicit focus on the context and challenges of each unique educational context. This model requires a significant degree of self-knowledge, or intrapersonal intelligence as understood by Gardner (1993). The notion of intrapersonal intelligence, along with interpersonal intelligence have formed the foundation for all the diverse theories of emotional intelligence (see, for example, Bar-On & Parker, 2000;

Goleman, 1995; Goleman & Boyatzis, 2008; Mayer & Salovey, 1997), which focus on making emotionally appropriate decisions and demonstrating emotionally intelligent behaviours, in this case, related to leadership decisions. Intrapersonal intelligence itself has two distinct aspects, both of which are critical to the process of personal reflection. One is simply knowledge of self and the other aspect relates executive function skills with an individual's personal capacity to understand and use these cognitive capacities to achieve their goals (Sellars, 2010, 2012).

The suite of cognitive capacities identified as executive function skills in Sellars (2010) include the complex interpolation of getting organised, initiating tasks, seeking feedback, inhibiting impulsive response, managing emotions, engaging positively, developing strong working memory, engaging with flexible thinking and following through with decisions, actions or plans despite distraction. Principals need to have sufficient self-knowledge in each of these components of executive function skills in order to engage effectively with the purpose, process and potential products or goals determined through engagement with the Personal Reflection Model. If an individual's understanding of their own values, beliefs and principles is not mediated by an authentic assessment of their capacity to employ each of the cognitive capacities of executive function skills, then the products, or goals of reflection, although appropriate and achievable, may easily not come to fruition. Table 1.1 offers a reflective process that combines the simplicity of Kolb's (1994) three-step model with sample questions that are provided to guide and facilitate customisation of the Personal Reflection Model to any situations, incidents or issues that may arise from the integration of students with refugee and asylum-seeker experiences.

### Research findings

While nearly every principal we spoke with articulated a method of reflection, there were two Australian principals, one primary and one secondary, whose stories were particularly noteworthy.

Context: This is now my 11th year at this school (K-6). This is a low SES school, high mobility, which means we have a very high turnover of students. I also experience high staff turnover now and then, which is pretty common for schools in our state. In terms of students, we have a whole lot coming from Syria.

*I'm always very careful. For example, because Anzac Day is something we do here at school, one of the traditions that I had before was I collect their ancestors' photos and we make a slideshow. I pop the kids up on the screen, so we can acknowledge their ANZAC heritage, and we acknowledge them as an ANZAC descendant. Now, we have started to look at those Australians that fought from different cultural backgrounds, and there's quite a few. I'm just mindful constantly of the changes in the school, of how we need to make this country everybody's country. Because it's really difficult; we have such an Australian tradition and that's a very strong Australian tradition. How do we*

*Table 1.1* A Personal Reflection Model

| Kolb (1994) | Questions related to self |
| --- | --- |
| *What?* | *Purpose*<br>What do I know?<br>Have I experienced discomfort about issues similar to this in the past?<br>What makes it important for me to consciously and purposefully think about this experience at this time? |
| *So What?* | *Process*<br>What is the focus here as I understand it?<br>Is there more than one level of reflection that I think needs to be considered as a focus for discussion in this experience?<br>In identifying my focus, what level(s) am I prioritising in my reflection? Why would I do that?<br>Do my priorities reflect my values and beliefs about the nature of my professional responsibilities with regard to integrating students with refugee and asylum-seeker experiences into my school community?<br>Do my priorities reflect anything about how I am developing as a school leader, integrating students with refugee and asylum-seeker experiences into my school community?<br>Do I need to engage at a level of reflection that necessitates engaging with ethical and moral considerations about policy, practices, behaviours or omissions on my part? |
| *Now What?* | *Product*<br>Do I need to take action or just think about what action may be appropriate if the circumstances permit?<br>Do I have the skills, knowledge and strategies to make a well-informed decision and take the action I have planned?<br>Can I realistically take action?<br>What personal, social and ideological influences have impacted on the action I plan to take?<br>How does my proposed action reflect my understanding and personal beliefs regarding what constitutes ethical, professional and effective leadership regarding the integration of students with refugee and asylum-seeker experiences?<br>Are my decisions and proposed actions congruent with my ethical and moral perspectives?<br>Do I have the executive function skills required to activate my plans successfully? |

(Adapted from Sellars, 2017, p. 13)

*manage that? For these kids that really haven't been here? What do we do? Some kind of a Fascist about what we can and can't, I don't know! There are things I'd like answers to that no one supports. Those occasions when we have Anzac Day and Remembrance Day, Australians feel very strongly about that.*

Context: Our school (Grades 7–12) has 1,200 students and I work in the Intensive English Centre with around 100 of those students. I have been doing this for 20 years. I've been working with kids from all different backgrounds for a long time, and I know what works.

*What we're finding is, the professional learning didn't have any impact until the teachers realised what they didn't know. At the start, they didn't know what they didn't know, they sort of realise, "Holy crap, we're going to have these kids in our class. We don't even know how to say their name, let alone spell it! Or what do we do if we're going to do sex ed? What do we do if we split into boys and girls' groups? We're doing World War II in and around history. What happens then?" We had to have an open-door policy down in the Intensive English Centre, where we take these questions all the time and when the teachers say listen, "I'm going to do this. What do you think?" So, there's a lot of checking in all the time with each other, which is really good. But I guess that's the hardest thing: getting people to understand that differentiation and knowing that we stand by whatever adjustment you make for an English-learner student will benefit your whole class.*

## Unique contexts, global principles

Each of the principals interviewed for this section were in the midst of working through a particularly discomforting situation. Though she presents as a very confident leader, the veteran primary principal was stepping carefully between celebrating Australia's Anzac Day (a remembrance of Australian wartime experiences) and being mindful of her many new students who bring with them horrific memories of war. More challenging, this principal is struggling with how she can include all her students and help make Australia everyone's country. The high school principal was focused on addressing the immense differences her newly arrived Middle Eastern students presented. She repurposed her school's Intensive English Centre to serve as a just-in-time helpdesk for her teachers, but, as the leader, she is still perplexed by numerous challenges. Specifically, she recognises that teaching sex education to mixed-gender classes containing her Islamic students could prove problematic and she is torn about the prospect of returning to gender-divided instruction – a practice her school already abandoned for pedagogical reasons. Unlike many vignettes presented throughout this book, these do not necessarily offer a resolution but rather a profile of principals engaged in purposeful reflection.

Reflection is messy business and for school leaders in the middle of addressing a challenge, having a framework or model to work through can be powerful. Though it can be tempting to react to challenges, leaders demonstrate care for their students and families by not responding reflexively to complex problems. Rather, reflective leaders understand there are many ways to alienate children and families with refugee and asylum-seeker experiences by making wrong decisions early. Sellars' (2017) Personal Reflection Model posits a series of questions at three levels to help define problems, identify processes for problem-solving and determine what, if any, types of actions to take. Valuable for conceptualising the parameters of the problem and the concerns of those involved, engaging at the *What* stage of the model may come easily to school leaders. It is at the *So What* stage where leaders often become bogged down in the process and where practice and collaboration are necessary. The *Now What* stage builds on the first two stages and ensures that actions put in place, if any, are more purposeful, thoughtful and comprehensive than would have been otherwise. Reflection does not ensure success, but it does ensure principals understand the challenges they are facing and can explain their responses to the people they serve.

## Chapter conclusion

School leaders driven by a desire to provide safe, caring, nurturing and inclusive learning environments for students and their families need to develop a process for reflection. The sheer demands of the role, the importance of education for all stakeholders, and the historical conventions of schooling which tend to replicate outdated policies and practices, each offer a reason for principals to become more thoughtful about how they face challenges and make decisions. Purposely designing schools that meet the needs of all stakeholders takes time and requires the development of reflective processes that become part of the culture. Supporting students and families with refugee and asylum-seeker backgrounds adds to this challenge but a purposeful reflective process offers a roadmap for more informed decision-making. When working with these families and students, this reflection spans a combination of cultural, academic, social, political, economic, racial and societal contexts, each with their own ways of deconstructing past and present realities and future opportunities. The challenge of effectively creating spaces of welcoming and safety for these individuals can be daunting. In this chapter, and throughout this book, school leaders demonstrate that reflection is not a clean or smooth process, but it is foundational for making informed decisions and meeting the needs of stakeholders. In Chapter 2, the caustic effects of racism on education are presented and the ways principals around the world reflect on and respond to racism are explored.

## References

Bar-On, R., & Parker, J. (2000). *The Handbook of Emotional Intelligence: Theory, Development, Assessment, and Application at Home, School, and in the Workplace*. Jossey-Bass.
Boyd, E. M., & Fales, A. W. (1983, April 1). Reflective learning: Key to learning from experience. *Journal of Humanistic Psychology*, 23(2), 99–117. doi:410.1177/0022167883232011.
Calderhead, J. (1989). Reflective teaching and teacher education. *Teaching and Teacher Education*, 5(1), 43–51. doi:10.1016/0742-051x(89)90018–90018.
Dewey, J. (1933). *How We Think: A Restatement of the Relation of Reflective Thinking to the Educative Process*. Heath.
Gardner, H. (1993). *Frames of Mind*. Tenth Anniversary Edition. Basic Books.
Goleman, D. (1995). *Emotional Intelligence: Why It Can Matter More Than IQ*. Bantam Books.
Goleman, D., & Boyatzis, R. (2008, Sept). Social intelligence and the biology of leadership. *Harvard Business Review*, 86(9), 74–81.
Gore, J. (1987). Reflecting on reflective teaching. *Journal of Teacher Education*, 38(2), 33–39. doi:10.1177/002248718703800208.

Gore, J., & Zeichner, K. (1991). Action research and reflective teaching in preservice teacher education: A case study from the United States. *Teaching and Teacher Education*, 7(2), 119–136. doi:10.1016/0742-051x(91)90022-h.

Kolb, D. (1994). *Experiential Learning: Experience as the Source of Learning and Development*. Prentice-Hall.

Leithwood, K., Sun, J., & Pollock, K. (Eds.). (2017). *How School Leaders Contribute to Student Success: The Four Paths Framework* (Vol. 23). Springer.

Mayer, J., & Salovey, P. (1997). What is emotional intelligence? In P. Salovey & D. Sluyter (Eds.), *Emotional Development and Emotional Intelligence: Educational Implications* (pp. 3–34). Basic Books.

Noffke, S., & Brennan, M. (1988). *The Dimensions of Reflection: A Conceptual and Contextual Analysis*American Educational Research Association, New Orleans.

Sellars, M. (2010). *Intrapersonal Intelligence, Executive Function and Stage Three Students* [Unpublished].

Sellars, M. (2012). Exploring executive function: Multiple intelligences' personalised mapping for success. *International Journal of Learning*, 18(3), 293–304. doi:10.18848/1447–9494/CGP/v18i03/47541.

Sellars, M. (2017). *Reflective Practice for Teachers*. Sage.

# 2 Racism

## Introduction

Every community has its own cultural norms, historical traditions and ways of engaging in the larger society that can ameliorate or perpetuate racism. This chapter focuses on one of the most complex issues school leaders face when children and families with refugee or asylum-seeker backgrounds join a school and larger school community. While school leaders are almost universally driven by a desire to create cultures of care and respect for difference, the challenge of confronting racism in all its forms and developing such cultures can seem daunting. To compound this challenge, many principals do not see themselves as community leaders as much as school leaders and are thus unsure how to address broader issues of racism that have a corrosive permeating effect on the school community. In this chapter, research on systemic racism, institutional racism and individual racism is explored and school leaders offer insights about mitigating the caustic effects of such racism.

## Systemic racism and governmentality

Systems engage with racist practices through policy making and its subsequent implementation, neither of which are attributable to the personal bias or prejudices of individuals. Instead, while they are developed in the best interests of those in power, Foucault (1991, 2003) indicates that he sees this as a strategic exercise. He discusses this racism as governmentality, excluding any influence or perception of personal opinion. He has a very specific notion of what he terms modern racism, indicating:

> The specificity of modern racism, or what gives it its specificity, is not bound up with mentalities, ideologies, or the lies of power. It is bound up with the technique of power, with the technologies of power ... the juxtaposition of – or the way biopower functions through old sovereign power of life and death implies the workings, the introduction and the activation of racism. And it is here I think that we find the roots of racism.
> (Foucault, 2003, p. 258)

DOI: 10.4324/9781003090731-2

While Foucault does not explain the exact relationship between biopower; the capacity to 'normalise' populations through data gathering and statistics; and governmentality, his idea of modern racism is intrinsically linked to both. Governmentality could be perceived as the gathering of data and statistics to improve the circumstances of groups of people, but it is important to understand the other purpose in which this information is utilised, especially in countries which have constantly changing policies and regulations in regard to those seeking asylum and refuge. Foucault (1991, p. 102) describes governmentality as: The ensemble formed by the institutions, procedures, analysis and reflections. The calculations and tactics that allow the exercise of this very specific; albeit complex form of power, which has as its target population, its principal form of knowledge, political economy, as its essential technological means, apparatuses of security.Rasmussen (2011, p. 40) describes this construct of Foucault's as 'flexible technology of power that entails a new and novel form of power'. This 'new and novel form of government' was distinguished by its capacity to differentiate between those individuals in society who were worthy of investment of resources, and those who were not. Those who were not assessed as worthy of societal resources such as education and health care were metaphorically left to be outsiders, to wither and die as they were to be denied the basic supports that would enable optimal human functioning. An example of this type of governmentality in action is the 'racist profiling' adopted by immigration officials in the United States which resulted in thousands of Americans being refused entry to their homeland (Samway et al., 2020), asylum-seeking and refugee mothers and their babies and children being sent to separate facilities, many of whom were subsequently deported without their children (Arar et al., 2020) and the 'hardening' of offshore processing, which resulted in individuals who had established their refugee status after being held in offshore Australian detention centres, but were never permitted to enter Australia (Refugee Council of Australia, 2020).

This type of exclusion and 'othering' is not new (Ball, 2012). It is just more readily facilitated on a wider scale than ever before with the computerisation of documentation, the data gathering facilitated by technology and the frequency and ease of policy change. The realities for principals is that, as part of their professional practice and accountability, they are responsible for contributing to this form of governmentality and to the type of normalising power that Foucault (1991) describes as 'biopower'. As already mentioned, biopower seeks to place everyone in society on a scale, a measure, chart or test from which a 'norm' can be calculated using data about all aspects of their lives and deaths. From this mathematical abstraction, everything that does not fit on the statistical 'curve' is regarded as abnormal. Officially validated as ensuring the health and wellbeing of entire populations, resistance to this type of power is extremely difficult in this technological age.

### Research findings

Many of our leaders raised concerns about the caustic effects of racism on children and families with refugee and asylum-seeker backgrounds. A high school principal in Australia and a high school principal in the United States shared important observations.

> Context: I've been here 13 years now as the boss. We have around 550 students and we're a very multicultural school. We are the place to put a lot of the refugee people. It seems like once you get a cultural group established, others want to come to that area because that's where they have those connections. I think our school population has around 90% non-English speaking background. We have about 60 different cultural groups across the schools. Arabic is the major language group, but we have multiple cultures within that language group.

> *I'd say there is still that band of racism and scepticism around refugees and asylum seekers. As a school, we get incredibly frustrated about our kids being cut out of opportunities by the general society. Look, even places like the local university have a very good program for trying to work with refugee people and kids and students and things like that. So, it's not that we don't feel supported. But all the stories you get, particularly the terrible way our government treats refugee people and calls them illegals. Just even the naming of it and things like that. That, if you're a refugee, to be called an illegal, is different. I'd be furious around that. So, I think there's a lot to be answered for in society.*

> Context: I've spent 19 years in education. The last seven or eight of those have been in administration at three different schools. My current school (Grades 9–12) is a high school with around 1,800 students. My current school has much fewer refugees than my previous school.

> *We aim to have very implicit scheduling and picking of students' classes to provide a support network of students who speak the same language or share a culture. The English Language Learning (ELL) teacher and the Teaching Assistant (TA), at least in schools in our area in the state, are just getting bombarded with caseload with not much support. I mean, it's not uncommon at all to see one ELL teacher and maybe a TA, and then they have a caseload near 100 or more students. And so, figuring out how to support these students has been critical pretty much in every school I have been in, because their numbers aren't really big enough to equal a cohort to count; as far as grading they exist in kind of a bubble outside of what the whole school is doing. At my old school we had a church that worked a lot with placement of these individuals, and we could count on them to be a partner to us, for example trying to get some parents in to be translators. At my current school, we have not had that same kind of community outreach partner, the kind of partner I think is really helpful. There's nothing in the county from the school side as a resource. We had to rely on the church who knew other people who would come from that community, other refugees who had come through kind of serve as guides for those parents, older siblings and the students that were coming in was critical.*

*Unique contexts, global principles*

When commenting on the diverse contexts and systems in which they are trying to support their students, each of our principals shared a great deal of frustration about broader issues outside of their control. The Australian principal has a wealth of in-school and community resources available to support his students with refugee and asylum-seeker backgrounds, including an engaged local university, but he is angered by his inability to counter a broader Australian narrative of his students being 'illegal'. This principal has made a conscious decision to leverage the resources available to him to support his students in spite of the wider system. Conversely, the US principal finds himself working in a community that is negative about the arrival of students with refugee backgrounds and a system that has not offered him the resources he needs to support his students. With an anaemic number of specialist staff members, this principal is struggling to offer his students the learning supports they desperately need. He has previously worked closely with the local religious communities to offset the deleterious effects of an education system that is both underserving and undervaluing his students. Each principal recognises the reality of systemic racism in the lives of their refugee and asylum-seeker students and each has found ways to mitigate its effects.

Schools do not exist as islands unto themselves. Rather, schools are part of education departments, communities, states and nations, and, as such, they are subjected to racist attitudes evident at each level. These attitudes are translated into policies and practices which act to limit the educational opportunities of students who are othered. Though many principals might assert that broader systemic issues are beyond their control, the principals we interviewed were clear about the need to identify and name this racism in order to address it. Analysing broader policies and resource allocations through the lens of specific groups of students can be a first step. The principal from the United States is a keen example of this, as he recognised his students with refugee and asylum-seeker backgrounds were not receiving equitable supports within a broader community that was unhappy with their presence. Just as he sought additional support from the local church, principals must figure out ways to work around systemic racism and its school-level effects that marginalise students with refugee and asylum-seeker backgrounds.

## Institutional racism

While institutions in society, such as schools, are governed by system-wide mandates and regulations, there are still opportunities for principals to develop and encourage policies, procedures and practices in their own contexts to identify, influence and minimise any potential situations in which racism may be experienced by members of the school community. Inherently different from the type of racism described by Foucault (1991), and Zizek (2008) who labelled racism as inflicted and perpetuated by those in authority as 'objective racism', the types of racism that are found in school contexts are readily influenced by the personal beliefs and values of the individuals who lead the school, namely the principals and their executive staff members. Brooks and Watson (2019) present an ecological approach to understanding racism in schools and developing appropriate relationships to circumvent incidences of this type of prejudice. They have identified five types of racism that may exist in school contexts. Dyadic racism investigates the ways in which principals develop positive relationships with the staff and community members and consequently influence their opinions and values. Working with the assumption that these principals are not racist themselves in their values and belief systems, it is an important aspect of the responsibilities undertaken by school leaders. These relationships are essentially the interaction between the principal and others individually. In this manner, the conversations and actions determined may have increased clarity of purpose, ethics and negotiation around philosophies and ideologies relating to the support of students with refugee and asylum-seeker experiences. Principals who wish to develop inclusive school communities, must, as the result of their interactions with their staff on the Emotional Path (Leithwood et al., 2017) (see also Chapter 9), find ways to engage in conversations about values and beliefs. In this way, the principal can personally contribute to the school developing and maintaining a shared vision of the foundational tenets of supporting these particular cohorts of students, despite their considerable degree of diversity.

Subcultural racism may still exist despite the positive leadership demonstrated by the principal. As the name indicates, it may develop in particular school sections or departments. These may be led by individuals who have resisted or disregarded the attempts of the principal to positively influence their attitudes and beliefs about the professional responsibility they have to attend to the rights and needs of students with refugee and asylum-seeker students. There is a greater likelihood of subcultural racism developing in large schools and those with distributed leadership models of governance (Harris et al., 2007). However, subcultural leadership may not just appear in the context of staff attitudes and values. Various groups of students in school contexts may share racist attitudes and opinions which are maintained despite the mainstream cultural orientation of the school and its articulated vision of inclusion and integration. These students may belong to discipline or house groups or be a subgroup of these, with or without any influence from the school leadership in those school departments. Institutional racism is found in school policies, procedures and general operating practices which do not offer equity of opportunity to all the students. This type of racism is frequently embedded in discipline policies which are not sensitive to the impact of trauma caused for these students as a result of forced migration, witnessing or suffering physical and emotional abuse, and the uncertainty of perilous and precarious journeys undertaken to settle in a new homeland.

Much of this lack of willingness to accommodate refugee and asylum-seeker students and deal with the impacts of trauma sensitively result in a disproportionally large percentage of these students being excluded from school (Carlile, 2012). Some of these policies and ways in which schools are organised and implemented are transparently racist, favourably biased towards one student cohort or prejudicial in favour of highly accomplished academic performance, an area in which students with refugee and asylum-seeker experiences cannot immediately complete. Others are more subtle or are racist by default. The ways in which equitable education is typically denied to students institutionally are the lack of consideration for first language and culture in the policies and procedures; little consideration of the psychological, cognitive and emotional needs of students who suffer from developmental or complex childhood trauma; and no attempt to consider other ways of doing and knowing as acceptable ontological epistemological beliefs and practices. This may be illustrated by the lack of sensitivity and the bullying nature of school authorities when dealing with the child and parents in the study discussed by Anders and Lester (2014, pp. 169–179). It is also demonstrated in the apparent absence of any recriminations from the school authorities when students in a German school actively and openly discriminated against a refugee student in their school (Anderson, 2001).

### Research findings

Across the world, many of our principals spoke with great passion about the need to advocate on behalf of students in the face of institutional racism. An Australian high school teacher and an Australian primary teacher shared powerful stories of addressing this racism.

> Context: Previously I've taught in various countries and in an International School for five years. My school has roughly 430 students, with close to 200 enrolled in an Intensive English Learning Centre as part of the school. At one point, we had 10% of all the asylum-seeker children in the state enrolled at this school.

> *Kids didn't want to go move to the mainstream school because they experienced racism while they were in the Intensive Centre (IC). It was sort of a structured institutional racism as well. In the mainstream school, for example, I found that the art teacher from the IC was walking around the school, carrying all her art materials in a little trolley until she found a classroom to teach art. But there were three fully equipped dark rooms and an art studio! So, I went to the guy who was in charge of art, and I said to him, "Why can't the art teacher from the Intensive Centre use the art rooms? Why is she forced to look for an ordinary classroom? And why can't she store her things in the art storeroom?" And he leaned back in a chair and, "oh, well," he said stretching back, "well, the IC doesn't share the philosophy of art that we have here at our school." That was a bit of a stunning statement. I mean, this is a serious issue. So, I said, "It is absolute bullshit and you will make available an art room to the IC teacher immediately and I expect that she will be able to use the art storeroom." He went on to hate me with undying hatred from that moment on.*

Context: I have a diverse background, having worked in behaviour consultancy and a number of diverse institutions prior to becoming a principal. My school (K-6) is an educational and community hub in a regional centre. For about three and a half years, our school had every newly arrived English as a Second Language (ESL) student in the region. Now, over 30% of our students are refugees.

*It all comes down to making our own system of thinking. Which completely changes everything because of the way it empowers your teachers not to seek approval, but to make the best decisions that they can for a student at any one time. You've got your fairness in terms of – fairness, not in terms of equality – fairness in terms of equity. At times this means tearing the system apart, in order to be able to actually refocus in on what is truly free and fair. So, there's a whole range of things: it's a lot of thinking, it's a lot of talking, it's a lot of debriefing people, it's a lot of making sure that there's some cognitive dissonance. That is what starts to break down barriers and get people to look at things in a slightly different way. It's really about the fact that you're making the best decisions for a person at any point in time. In this, there is a consistency in the fact that you're making those best decisions. You need to trust in developing it, because it's not defined by something outside of what we do.*

### Unique contexts, global principles

Despite vastly different approaches to leading, each of these principals recognises the importance of identifying and breaking down systems and practices that promote institutional racism. The high school principal from Australia was relatively new to her position when she recognised subcultural racism was limiting the academic opportunities of her students with refugee and asylum-seeker experiences. The art teacher used a difference in 'philosophy' as a way to construct a barrier to keep teachers and students away from the school's art facilities. Assertive by nature, this principal both demolished the barrier and sent a signal to her stakeholders about serving students ahead of addressing inequitable policies – real or perceived. Our primary principal shared insights about how he operates on a daily basis. Keenly focused on developing the confidence and capacity of his teachers to make the best possible decisions they can in any situation, this principal engages his staff in frequent dialogue. Deeply reflective, this principal works hard to help his teachers recognise detrimental classroom and school policies often founded on notions of equality instead of equity, practices that may harm or disadvantage certain groups of students. Both principals have developed an environment in which their teachers understand that school conventions and policies are only valuable to the point where they harm students.

Creating school environments in which all educators feel empowered to identify and challenge detrimental policies is a lofty goal for principals. In fact, for many principals, the idea of empowering individual teachers to challenge policies can be unsettling. But, as the experiences of our two leaders illustrate, principals must initiate and support this work. In some cases, this leadership is abrupt and decisive, but mostly it is thoughtful and methodical. Faced with a grossly unfair situation, our high school leader chose to stand on principle and dismantle a racist institutional policy. Her stance clarified for any in doubt about her value system and priorities. Our primary principal illustrates someone who Brooks and Watson (2019) would contend works to impact the thinking, values and approach of his staff through purposeful dialogue around problems of practice. Helping his teachers create their own systems of thinking empowers them to make decisions with student equity in mind. In fact, this approach is the evolution of empowerment, as it offers teachers a framework for identifying systemic racism around them and encourages them to pull those systems apart. School leaders willing to educate and empower their staff members to dismantle systemic racism are setting their schools on a trajectory to meeting the needs of every student.

## Individual and societal racism

Aguayo (2019) discusses race and whiteness in Castagno (2014) as frameworks used in education to perpetuate the existing structures and the ideals of those in power, explaining that white school leaders with 'good' intentions use good manners and politeness to perpetuate the ever-present racial inequity in societies as an accepted and acceptable fact of everyday life. Brisco (2013) notes that it is only a process of transformative leadership in which school leaders 'deconstruct' their notions of self and engage in change at a deeply personal level that has the potential to combat racism and racist behaviours at a school level. Edgeworth (2013) discusses the problem of two students of colour in an all-white rural environment and Fuller-Hamilton (2019) discusses the barriers that curtail confronting conversations on racism and the ways in which oppression is sustained as neutrality, colour blindness and institutional racism. None of these authors question the development of racist attitudes and actions permitting those who would perpetuate it, by omission or by nuanced commitment, to escape from rationalising, justifying or simply examining the grounds on which their prejudices or lack of action are founded. Kendi (2017) argues that it is not ignorance or fear that perpetuates racism but the compelling impact of self-interest which allows injustices and atrocities to flourish in society without official comment or commitment to change.

Brooks and Watson (2019) contend that racial views, prejudices and bias are developed from a very young age, initially in the home. Children are influenced by the opinions they hear being justified, by media exposure and, later, by personal experiences and perceptions of self-identity as whiteness. Personal experiences are important as racist views are typically based on negative thoughts or feelings about another's personal attributes, which are then generalised to be an individual's generally held perceptions of everyone who fits into that group. Prejudice and bias can be focused on a number of different attributes which make the individual to whom the prejudicial views and actions

are directed different to those holding the prejudice. There may be one particular difference, in this case racial origins, but these frequently are exacerbated
by the differences in which diverse ethnic groups dress, worship and raise the
children with various expectations and practices. Prejudicial beliefs are illogical,
baseless in that they are not founded in logic or reason and, while they may be
exaggerated by personal experiences, when they are then focused on all the
members of a specific group, totally inequitable. Equally nonsensical and
unreasonable is to group people according to one or two characteristics. Individuals organise themselves in a variety of diverse ways, using different criteria
in disparate contexts and situations (Ladson-Billings & Tate, 2009).

It is individuals who make up societies. Those who are like-minded in prejudicial ways typically (Berry, 2009, pp. 361–371) come together and perpetuate these biases, creating a shared, communally acceptable view of specific
groups of people who are collectively thought to be 'lesser' than themselves.
When this type of thinking becomes acceptable in any societal group, including
the wider school community, then major and minor aggressions against groups
or individual students with specific characteristics are dismissed or considered to
be acceptable. Equally important is an understanding of racism or 'unbelonging'
attitudes and actions which are permissible as the result of an individual's lack of
commitment to challenging these injustices and baseless opinions. This may be
a common situation in school contexts where teachers and others with
authority ignore many behaviours which could reasonably be perceived to be
racist in nature. Many of these issues may present as bullying behaviours which
require sensitive and conscientious consideration by school leaders. The incidents of bullying experienced by students with refugee and asylum-seeker
experiences are well documented (for example, Alivernini et al., 2019;
Mthethwa-Sommers & Kisiara, 2015; Walsh et al., 2015) and many are extremely explicit (Anderson, 2001; Baak, 2019; Blackwell & Melzak, 2000; Carlile,
2012; Corbett et al., 2014; Mengesha et al., 2017; Schroeter & James, 2015).
These behaviours not only distress students at the time, but negatively impact
on the damage (cognitive, emotional social and developmental) that is the
result of the students' exposure to extreme trauma before, during and after
displacement and in the difficulties of resettlement (Bonanno, 2004; Hart,
2009; Miller et al., 2018).

### Research findings

A handful of the principals we interviewed talked of overt racism directed
towards newly arrived families with refugee and asylum-seeker backgrounds. A
primary principal from Northern Ireland and a high school principal from
Australia each offered a unique vantage point on the problem.

> Context: Our school has been around for close to a century and was ori-
> ginally set up to serve the local population. When I began here 15 years
> ago, the population was mostly local. But now, we're around 80% English

as an Additional Language (EAL). That's been over the past 10 years that it has grown. We have learnt along the way, and it's been a process that has evolved over the last 10 years.

*Strangers are not always made welcome in the area and anyone who is deemed to be behaving in an anti-social manner, who isn't a local, is punished or intimidated out of the area. When we started to enrol more refugees and asylum-seeker pupils, many local parents moved their children to other schools in the area. They made many excuses to us, but when I spoke to the principal of the other school, the reasons were purely racist. A local City Councillor took great glee in informing me that our school was known in the village as "Africa School." If our local elected representatives had that attitude, we knew that we had a battle on our hands. So, we had and still have, a mix of children with a lot of issues. The local children suffer from what we call the 'legacy' issues of the Troubles and many of our EAL population have been through unspeakable trauma in their own countries and have then suffered the indignities and uncertainties to actually reach safety. Even when they have managed to reach our city, they face the uncertainty of whether they will be allowed to stay.*

Context: I've lived my whole life here. I was born in this town: school, university, the whole thing. I have been a school principal for nearly 20 years. I've been working with kids from all different backgrounds for a long time, and I know what works. In our school (Years 7–12) we have about 1,200 students and around 250 of those students identify as Aboriginal. We have an Intensive English Centre now, which is very new. We have around 100 students who all identify as Yazidi.

*I think initially there was a little bit of pushback in town around the arrival of Yazidi people. Here at the school, we did have some issues with our Aboriginal students and their interactions with Yazidi kids. It had a sense of almost a competitiveness in terms of disadvantage, and that sounds dreadful, but that's how it was expressing itself. The Aboriginal kids here were kind of used to being the most disadvantaged within the school. Suddenly, we've got some new people that have come from pretty tricky backgrounds. It was even to the point where some of the parents within the Aboriginal Educational Consultative Group were questioning the amount of funding that goes into the new arrivals program. They were sort of insinuating that maybe some of the money that was destined for their students might have been being redirected towards our refugee kids. So yes, so there's just been that little bit of tension.*

## Unique contexts, global principles

The context, history and culture of any school has a great bearing on how its staff, students and community react to change. As the narratives of our two principals illustrate, the arrival of children and families with refugee and asylum-seeker backgrounds can yield unpleasant reactions. Passionate in his approach, the primary principal from Northern Ireland is navigating a situation in which community prejudices were historically focused on religious differences and the arrival of non-white students has sent many of his families to other schools. The words of the local councillor capture this pervasive racism and this principal recognises that he must battle to maintain his integrity and garner community support. The secondary principal from Australia has a very different issue on her hands, which is again rooted in the context of her school. Optimistic and thoughtful, this principal is dealing with a historically marginalised group that is vocal in their opposition to the perceived sharing of resources with students recognised to be outsiders. These local students, in fact, have created an identity around the idea of being the most disadvantaged and the newly arrived students are threatening this standing. Both principals are cognisant of the individual and societal racism that is playing out in and around their schools. This awareness is the springboard for each principal to address this situation.

It may seem counter-intuitive, but the fact that people have suffered from prejudice and racism does not necessarily make them more sensitive to the plight of others. There is no automatic sense of empathy that comes from having been marginalised. This is illustrated in our school examples of Aboriginal families who have suffered horrific racism for generations and Northern Irish citizens who have experienced violent racism founded on religion. When a critical mass of people in a community create a sense of what is acceptable, racism can flourish and those who remain silent are complicit in this racism. Our primary school in Northern Ireland dubbed 'Africa School' is a prime example of a community that has allowed racism to grow and has placed the principal in a precarious position. This principal is vocal in his disdain for such racism and he leads with bravery and integrity. The arrival of others is often seen as creating competition for resources, as our Australian high school situation demonstrates. This principal is active in her efforts to ensure that every one of her students has the resources he or she needs. Our systems are often set up against outsiders and it takes principals willing to work within and up against policies to make a difference for all students.

## Chapter conclusion

Racism and its effects can take on many forms in schools. In some cases, racism is highly visible and confronting and, in other more common situations, it is nearly invisible, wrapped into long-standing policies and practices that marginalise groups of students or families. Principals must work to identify racism in their schools and communities, and they need to create a culture of staff, students and community members who push back against it. For principals who are working with traditionally marginalised populations or in communities that have a history of racial unrest, it is important they do not assume such experiences will yield a more understanding, more empathetic or less racist community. Communities determine what is acceptable through their actions and principals have a unique vantage point to challenge, shape and influence community behaviour through the values they promote and the actions they take within their schools. These actions should be informed through a reflective process, as discussed in Chapter 1. Reflection is an integral component of meeting the challenges of racism and building a vibrant learning community. In Chapter 3, the opportunities of cultural diversity to enhance a school's direction for the future are explored.

## References

Aguayo, D. (2019). Dismantling racism in public schools using critical race theory and Whiteness Studies. *Urban Education*, 54(5), 764–771.

Alivernini, F., Manganelli, S., Cavicchiolo, E., & Lucidi, F. (2019). Measuring bullying and victimization among immigrant and native primary school students: Evidence from Italy. *Journal of Psychoeducational Assessment*, 37(2), 226–238. doi:10.1177/0734282917732890.

Anders, A. D., & Lester, J. N. (2014). Navigating authoritarian power in the United States: Families with refugee status and allegorical representation. *Cultural Studies, Critical Methodologies*, 15(3), 169–179. doi:10.1177/1532708614565453.

Anderson, P. (2001). 'You don't belong here in Germany...' On the social situation of refugee children in Germany. *Journal of Refugee Studies*, 14(2), 187–199.

Arar, K., Orucu, D., & Waite, D. (2020). Understanding leadership for refugee education: Introduction to the special issue. *International Journal of Leadership in Education: Theory and Practice*, 23(1), 1–6. doi:10.1080/13603124.2019.1690958.

Baak, M. (2019). Racism and Othering for South Sudanese heritage students in Australian schools: Is inclusion possible? *International Journal of Inclusive Education*, 23(2), 125–141. doi:10.1080/13603116.2018.1426052.

Ball, S. (2012). *Foucault, Power, and Education*. Taylor & Francis.

Berry, J. (2009). A critique of critical acculturation. *International Journal of Intercultural Relations*, 33(5), 361–371. doi:10.1016/j.ijintrel.2009.06.003.

Blackwell, D., & Melzak, S. (2000). *Far from the Battle but Still at War: Troubled Refugee Children in School*. Child Psychotherapy Trust.

Bonanno, G. A. (2004). Loss, trauma, and human resilience: Have we underestimated the human capacity to thrive after extremely aversive events? *American Psychologist*, 59(1), 20–28. doi:10.1037/0003-066X.59.1.20.

Brisco, P. (2013, July). Developing transformative leaders to support everyday antiracism practices. Canadian Journal of Educational Administration and Policy, Issue no. 142, 134–159.

Brooks, J., & Watson, T. (2019). School leadership and racism: An ecological perspective. *Urban Education*, 54(5), 631–655. doi:10.1177/0042085918783821.

Carlile, A. (2012). An ethnography of permanent exclusion from school: Revealing and untangling the threads of institutionalised racism. *Race Ethnicity and Education*, 15(2), 175–194. doi:10.1080/13613324.2010.548377.

Castagno, A. (2014). *Educated in Whiteness: Good Intentions and Diversity in Schools*. University of Minnesota Press.

Corbett, E., Gunasekera, H., Maycock, A., & Isaacs, D. (2014). Australia's treatment of refugee and asylum seeker children: The views of Australian paediatricians. *The Medical Journal of Australia*, 201(7), 389–393.

Edgeworth, K. (2013). *Refugees in Rural Schools: Issues of Space, Racism and (Un) Belonging.* Australian Association for Research in Education Conference, Adelaide, South Australia.

Foucault, M. (1991). Governmentality. In B. Burchell, G. Gordon, & B. Miller (Eds.), *The Foucault Effect: Studies in Governmentality* (pp. 87–104). Chicago University Press.

Foucault, M. (2003). 'Society must be defended' (D. Macey, Trans.). In *Lectures at the Collège de France 1975–1976*. Picador.

Fuller-Hamilton, A. (2019). The circular conversation around racism and the actions necessary for racial change. *Urban Education*, 54(5), 760–763.

Harris, A., Leithwood, K., Day, C., Sammons, P., & Hopkins, D. (2007). Distributed leadership and organizational change: Reviewing the evidence. *Journal of Educational Change*, 8, 337–347.

Hart, R. (2009). Child refugees, trauma and education: Interactionist considerations on social and emotional needs and development. *Educational Psychology in Practice*, 25(4), 351–368. doi:10.1080/02667360903315172.

Kendi, I. (2017). *Stamped from the Beginning: The Definitive History of Racist Ideas in America.* Nation Books: A Member of the Perseus Books Group.

Ladson-Billings, G., & Tate, W. (2009). Towards a critical race theory of education. In A. Darder, M. Baltodamao, & R. Torres (Eds.), *The Critical Pedagogy Reader* (pp. 167–182). Routledge.

Leithwood, K., Sun, J., & Pollock, K. (Eds.). (2017). *How School Leaders Contribute to Student Success: The Four Paths Framework* (Vol. 23). Springer.

Mengesha, Z. B., Perz, J., Dune, T., & Ussher, J. (2017). Refugee and migrant women's engagement with sexual and reproductive health care in Australia: A socio-ecological analysis of health care professional perspectives. *Plos One*, 12(7), e0181421. doi:10.1371/journal.pone.0181421.

Miller, E., Ziaian, T., & Esterman, A. (2018). Australian school practices and the education experiences of students with a refugee background: A review of the literature. *International Journal of Inclusive Education*, 22(4), 339–359. doi:10.1080/13603116.2017.1365955.

Mthethwa-Sommers, S., & Kisiara, O. (2015). Listening to students from refugee backgrounds: Lessons for education professionals. *Perspectives on Urban Education*, 12 (1). https://files.eric.ed.gov/fulltext/EJ1056671.pdf.

Rasmussen, K. (2011). Foucault's genealogy of racism. *Theory, Culture & Society*, 28(5), 34–51.

Refugee Council of Australia. (2020, May 20). *Australia's offshore processing regime: The facts.* www.refugeecouncil.org.au/offshore-processing-facts/.

Samway, K., Pease-Alvarez, L., & Alverez, L. (2020). *Supporting Newcomer Students: Advocacy and Instruction for English Learners.* W.W. Norton & Company.

Schroeter, S., & James, C. E. (2015). "We're here because we're Black": The schooling experiences of French-speaking African-Canadian students with refugee backgrounds. *Race Ethnicity and Education*, 18(1), 20–39. doi:10.1080/13613324.2014.885419.

Walsh, S., Clercq, B., Molcho, M., Harel-Fisch, Y., Davison, C. M., Madsen, K. R., & Stevens, G. W. J. M. (2015). The relationship between immigrant school composition, classmate support and involvement in physical fighting and bullying among adolescent immigrants and non-immigrants in 11 countries. *Journal of Youth and Adolescence*, 45(1), 1–16. doi:10.1007/s10964-015-0367-0.

Zizek, S. (2008). *Violence.* Profile Books Ltd.

# 3   Understanding cultural diversity

## Introduction

Each child comes to school with unique life experiences, cultural traditions, familial practices and ethnic background that shape who they are and how they interact with their world. How schools handle cultural difference affects the wellbeing of the entire school community and individual student learning outcomes. Children with refugee and asylum-seeker backgrounds likely come with very different cultures and experiences compared to students from the host community. This can create opportunities for building bridges across differences OR promote narrow-minded values of the status quo culture to dominate and inhibit building a caring learning community for all. School leaders must strive to understand as much as they can about the journeys, beliefs, special gifts, opportunities, challenges (including traumas) and values children with refugee and asylum-seeker backgrounds bring to their schooling. The purposeful effort to understand, reflect upon, incorporate and celebrate each student is foundational to creating welcoming environments. This chapter offers research on multiple ways of knowing and understanding individuals from different backgrounds. Research with principals is also presented and analysed regarding the imperative of recognising culture and incorporating it into the growth of a school.

## Culture and Hall's iceberg

Everyone has culture. Everyone has ethnicity. The two are invariably intertwined by all individuals living in societies and aspects of these can arouse varying degrees of emotional response. This is because they represent beliefs, values and perspectives which are then integrated in ways that support identity formation, both in forms of self-identity and identification with others of the same cultural and ethnic groups. It is rare that any individual, however isolated from others, would find themselves not identifying with the customs and practices of any social group. Culture, however, is complex and has frequently been likened to an iceberg, much of which remains hidden under a relatively unimposing visible exterior. The first of these cultural iceberg models has been

DOI: 10.4324/9781003090731-3

attributed to Hall (1976). Despite the decades since publication, his model is still used effectively in many areas of life including education (see, for example, Thier, 2013). Hall posited that the 10% of the iceberg that is visible above the waterline is representative of the aspects of culture that are also apparent in populations. In this first section of the iceberg, Hall indicates that observable behaviours such as language, national dress and festivals, food choices and preparation, creative works such as art, music, dramatic works and literature and other nationalistic icons and symbols are those which elicit the least emotional intensity for most people as they are overt, explicitly learned, public in nature and unquestionably associated with the national identity that each individual understands to be their community. They are not behaviours that regularly challenge those of other cultures and are generally a source of pride and common understandings despite being changeable and organic, as are all social systems. These cultural characteristics are frequently the avenues through which education systems seek to acknowledge diversity in their school communities and to introduce an understanding of the various cultural ways of communication, celebration and expression. These celebrations, however, like the iceberg itself, present a tiny percentage of cultural differences and beliefs and, when planned as isolated recognition of community diversity, are frequently regarded as tokenism and not as an acceptance and consideration of various ways of doing and understanding across the mainstream of school life.

> Tokenistic practices include the occasional introduction of multicultural songs, the display of diverse languages or national flags, and the celebration of some cultural festivals. When multicultural situations are handled in a tokenistic way, there is (albeit unintentionally) only superficial respect for diverse cultural practices, and families and children of minority cultures have limited access to their cultural values.
>
> (Hargraves, 2019, p. 1)

The next 10% of the iceberg represents what Hall (1976) identifies as 'shallow' culture and includes the more nuanced behaviours of social interactions. These include aspects of direct communication such as eye contact, notions of exhibiting emotions appropriately, perceptions of personal space and body contact such as hand shaking and hugging, and interpretations of body language. The latter includes facial expression, modal expression and tone of voice. This level includes relationship dynamics including perceptions of beauty, appropriateness of interactions and associations, leadership and decision-making. It also relates to intensely personal but visible behaviours such as child-rearing customs, notions and expectations of adolescence, expectations of hygiene and cleanliness and perspectives relating to the criticality of illness and disease. Emotional intensity at this level is high, which may be anticipated as these behaviours, while observable, are not as visible as the surface cultural characteristics but are related to the ways in which personal and social ways of interacting and making meaning are understood as appropriate, despite frequently remaining unspoken. The remainder of the iceberg is focused on the implicitly learned, unconscious behaviours which carry an intense emotional load. These reflect deeply established values and beliefs which are often not negotiable, including notions of obscenity, familial roles of responsibilities and relationships of parents and dependents, self-identity, tolerance of hardship and suffering, and established characteristics of societies in which the individuals and the forebears have been immersed over a long period of time. These latter characteristics include views relating to compliance and competition, power distance in social status and occupations, male and female roles in society, and outlooks on past, present and future which govern how they perceive life in general. Each of these levels of culture may impact on the ways in which schools with refugee and asylum-seeker students and their communities interact, interpret and integrate with their school communities in contexts which differ from the ontological frameworks of their original homelands.

## Research findings

Many of our participants shared insights on the importance of recognising the cultures from which their students come. Of note were the observations of a primary school principal in Australia and a secondary educator in New Zealand.

> Context: I have been the principal here for 18 months. Prior to coming to this school, I didn't understand the complexity of it and how special it is. It's such a special place, it really makes me – as a leader – be so humble and grateful. Currently in our school we have roughly 200 students. In our student population, 70% of children are English as Second Language or Dialect. We have 12 or 13 languages that are spoken within our school. We have a really diverse community. Those children are from families who are asylum seekers, refugees, and some have parents that are here doing their PhD. But there is a lot of trauma for most of the children.

> *It's not just the kids, it goes to the family as well. I had one mom that said, "if they misbehave just smack them." And I said, "We don't smack in Australia. This is the expectation that we have in our school system." And the mom was explaining to me, in her country, that children are smacked when they misbehave. So even just showing them, that's okay in your country but in our country, we don't do that. I went through the wellbeing policy with her: explaining what my role as a principal is and what her role was, as a mom. We do touch on culture; we try and bring culture in the depth of the curriculum. We try to link into their home country. A lot of them, they're missing their home country, they've come without family members and they still want that connection to home, so we try to get that through. We have a lot of families that come with that, because their dads... because they don't know where their dads are. We try to talk them through that. We have a school counsellor that talks to them around that and how that can happen in Australia too. We have other families here that don't have dads and we are just trying to make those similarities and comparisons.*

Context: We have roughly 1,400 students from Years 9 to 13 (ages 13 to 18). Thirteen or fourteen years ago was when we had our first former refugee students from Eritrea. When refugees come, they actually get placed according to the housing available. So, in our area there was a lot of housing at quite a low cost; a lot of refugee families got put into this area and they developed communities. For example, there's quite an established Congolese community and quite an established Burmese or Myanmar community.

*We used to have dinners where we would give the families money. They would use it to buy ingredients for their own food and then they'd bring along their food and their families and the community people. It would be really helpful for the principal to meet the families to build confidence for those families and their confidence in liaising with the school. So, also that way, the principal got to know the families, and gain an understanding of racism, bullying, and actually realising that is not made up. Gaining an understanding of microaggressions and dealing with it on a schoolwide thing.*

### Unique contexts, global principles

Each of our principals understand the importance of developing relationships with, and acknowledging the cultural values of, their newly arrived families. Our primary principal addressed acceptable punishment with one family by acknowledging the difference in child-rearing attitudes and values between Australia and the family's home country. Most western countries now focus on psychological measures for dealing with student behaviour, focusing on self-regulation and having students take responsibility for their own actions. This is not an approach that many of the newly arrived families in this school may recognise or understand. This principal chose to recognise but challenge this family's beliefs by sharing the policy and helping the parents see the benefits for their child. Our New Zealand leader had a strategic approach to involving parents in the school environment. Providing her families with money to purchase and share their home country's food sent a message that their culture is valued. Through these special school-based dinners, this principal recognised difference and brought families into the school community. These events also enabled this principal to learn of the challenges her newly arrived families were experiencing. Both principals have engaged in sometimes difficult dialogue and effort to help their children and families with refugee and asylum-seeker backgrounds feel part of the school culture.

For principals to create environments where newly arrived families feel welcome, they must lead with a recognition that the families are likely markedly different from those of the host country. These families hold a worldview and possess values that are, in many cases, radically different from those of their new neighbours. Principals need to look beyond these differences and identify ways to respect and dignify families with refugee and asylum-seeker experiences. Bringing these families into school communities and letting them access things that they may never have experienced or even thought of is pivotal. Schools that promote personalisation, student choice, alternative assessment and progressive values may, in some cases, be a very new reality for these families. Our leaders spoke about managing the communication channels for different ways that school is run in the West. They are focused on developing trust and a sense of community and to do this requires a willingness to listen, to be accepting but also to be assertive when necessary.

## Culture and Hofstede's societal differences

While Hall (1976) developed a cultural iceberg to demonstrate cultural differences in communicating and other associated aspects of personal difference, Hofstede (2001; Hofstede et al., 2010) investigated major dimensions of societies. Defined as an aspect of a culture, his dimensions were established to explain various characteristics of national cultures, while acknowledging that with any culture there would be individual perspectives and personal attributes that did not necessarily identify with the cultural dimensions that were attributed to their national culture. Initially, Hofstede et al.'s (2010) work discussed four dimensions of culture. A fifth dimension was added as the result of Minkov et al. (2018) and his colleagues. A sixth dimension was also added to provide a more comprehensive understanding of the nature of societies when compared to each other. These are currently the dimensions with which Hofstede et al. (2010, p. 8) engage in their comparison of cultural dimensions:

1   Power Distance, related to the different solutions to the basic problem of human inequality;
2   Uncertainty Avoidance, related to the level of stress in a society in the face of an unknown future;
3   Individualism versus Collectivism, related to the integration of individuals into primary groups;
4   Masculinity versus Femininity, related to the division of emotional roles between women and men;
5   Long Term versus Short Term Orientation, related to the choice of focus for people's efforts: the future or the present and past;
6   Indulgence versus Restraint, related to the gratification versus control of basic human desires related to enjoying life.

The first of these dimensions, Power Distance, refers to the degree to which life is acknowledged as an unequal balance of power. Societies which have high degrees of power distance accept that power does not need to be legitimised, those who are subordinate are expected to obey unquestionably, the country's income is unevenly distributed, and that corruption is rampant, but scandal must be avoided. Elders are both respected and feared, children are taught total obedience, and education systems are invariably teacher orientated. Many of these societies have religious traditions which are intrinsically hierarchical. In incidents of low degrees of power distance, the opposites are found. Power must be legitimised and is expected to be used for good, subordinates expect to be consulted, hierarchies reflect increasing responsibilities and different roles, governments are more democratic, and scandals can ruin careers. Parents consult and consider options with their children and pedagogical strategies are more student centred.

These contrasting views are provided for each of the dimensions, and may easily explain the confusion, disbelief, dismay or incredulity that is experienced by members of communities who have refugee and asylum-seeker backgrounds and are enrolling their children and young people into schools which are situated in societies with very different cultural dimensions. Behaviours exhibited by individuals from societies which have strong uncertainty avoidance dimensions may include increased anxiety and stress about any type of ambiguity or difference. They may expect rigorous rules, clear frameworks and have expectations that teachers have the answers to everything. They may regard diverse ideas and behaviours as dangerous. Individuals from collectivist societies are unwaveringly loyal to their families or clans; they avoid using language in which they express personal opinion as they prefer harmony of group consensus to individual perspectives and opinions. Other individuals may be classified as in the group or out of the group, high importance is placed on belonging and relationships take precedence over tasks. Educational purpose is perceived to be learning 'how to do', not learning how to think.

One of the challenges for schools who welcome students with refugee and asylum-seeker experiences may be the views of parent communities who originate from societies with high feminine dimensions. In these communities both genders are expected to be kind and caring, both parents discuss facts and feelings with their children, there is a balance between family and work life, and both girls and boys, while permitted to cry, should not fight. Sex is considered to be a way of relating and mothers determine how many children a couple may have. These expectations and dimensional characteristics may be confrontational in societies where girls can cry but boys cannot, boys should fight but girls should not; there is excessive admiration for the strong and males are expected to exhibit this characteristic. It may also cause difficulties around discussion of sexuality which are subject to moralistic values and beliefs.

The implications of cohorts of school communities who are from societies with dimensions of short-term orientations are most importantly around success or failure at school, which these students may attribute to luck, their tendency to look backwards for significant events and their relatively blind adhesion to tradition and their strict family lives. They may be predisposed to consumerism yet value their country above all others and be committed to service to others without thoughtful planning for the future, fiscal and otherwise. The final dimension reports on the dimension relating to indulgence and restraint. Individuals from restrained societies may experience or remember fewer positive experiences than in indulgent societies and have fewer happy people. They may exhibit behaviours of helplessness, of having no control, or take no responsibility for what is happening in their lives, not value free speech and they may be reluctant to participate in sporting and leisure activities. They are frequently associated with countries which have high levels of police control, restricted birth numbers and fewer obese people, despite food being plentiful. The hugely diverse contexts, national cultures and personal circumstances from which students with refugee and asylum-seeker experiences originate may be extremely complex, but an understanding of cultural dimensions has the potential to make school-based interactions more positive and productive and to influence the decision-making of principals.

### Research findings

Our participants identified disconnects in expectations and lived experiences between host communities and families from other societies. Of note were the observations of a primary school principal in Australia and a secondary principal in Australia.

> Context: My school is a small school, with students in kindergarten to Year 6. We are a community hub in the inner city. A range of consultants and support teachers are based at the school. We celebrate our unique and diverse population at the school, with over 30% of our students arriving as refugees from around the globe. We also provide regional assistance through a support class for students that have a mild intellectual disability.

> *Number one, go and do some research. And that research is whatever you can learn about different cultures. What's happened, the wars, everything that has occurred, go and read as much as you can. But then go and do things: go and visit the local mosque, go and visit that mosque and go and ask some questions. So, you're in dialogue and you actually start to understand on a really deep level, because until you understand things to the deep level you can't build trust. Still, when you know things sometimes one single little mistake can erode all the trust that you've built.*

> Context: I've been here for two years. This school is a 7–12 school, we have an 80% EALD background, which means non-English speaking. We also have an Intensive English Centre of about 150 students, which comprises refugee international students and new arrivals. A lot of them have come from war-torn countries and come to us with extreme trauma from places like Syria, Afghanistan, Iraq. We have lots of students, also, from China. A lot of them have been refugees within their own countries, and many of them have not accessed education until they arrive in Australia.

> *You hear from these kids their stories and it's just, it's amazing. It's beyond belief. They'll tell you the story, that dad has tried three times to come on the boat. Kids will tell you about their parents, who are still missing in the country that they left, or*

*how the house has been bombed three times by the Americans. Or that they didn't get to say goodbye to anyone because if they said goodbye, there's a chance they could be kidnapped and held for ransom. They had to be careful about playing as after all, in their country, they think parents are rich if the children can afford to play. These are all the stories that come out but listening to the kids and you can see the healing that happens as a result of that, it's pretty special I have to say. Yes, look; we've got so much to offer. It's really good. Yes, we get to make a real difference. So many of our kids say thank you, they say thank you to me daily and half the time I can't believe they are thanking me for these things, saying thanks for the furniture.*

### Unique contexts, global principles

Both of our principals talked extensively about the importance of authentically learning about the students and families they serve. Our Australian primary principal is sensitive to the idea that relationships take a long time to develop and little mistakes can undermine trust. As such, he is a proponent of seeking information about his refugee and asylum-seeker families from multiple sources, including the local mosque. Purposeful in his approach, this principal continuously engages in dialogue with his teachers, families and community members to understand all he can and respond sensitively to the unique aspects of his students' cultures. Our high school principal spends much time in dialogue with her students. She knows their stories; she understands their resilience and is cognisant of their capacity to recover from great trauma. She recognises that her newly arrived students are still living with the experiences and expectations of their home cultures, as evidenced by her observation about play. This principal's observation that her students could not play in their home countries for fear of being perceived as wealthy and thus become a potential kidnapping victim represents her understanding of the many degrees of difference she is removed from their reality. Understanding how to respond to the lived experiences of refugee and asylum-seeker students does not necessarily come naturally to empathetic and caring leaders. Each of our principals stressed the need to learn widely, to ask questions, to listen and reflect.

For students and families with refugee and asylum-seeker backgrounds, the move from their home countries to their new countries is far more than a geographic leap. As Hofstede et al. (2010, p. 8) identify, the move can bring massive cultural shifts affecting nearly all aspects of life. School leaders must recognise that their newly arrived students will live in two worlds for a period of time and it is imperative to be accommodating in order to help these students become integrated. It is not the role of schools to assimilate these students; rather, committed principals need to find ways to understand and honour their students' first culture. Our two principals went to great extents to seek understandings about their students' cultures and our vignettes show the power and potential of this learning. Children with refugee and asylum-seeker backgrounds have the capacity, perhaps more than other children, to appreciate the benefits of attending school. Listening to them, thinking about expectations and ways of doing in their home cultures, being sensitive to issues of power difference and male and female cultural roles are foundational actions to building a welcoming school environment.

## Culture and microsystems

Hall (1976) discussed many of the personal beliefs and mores of communication from an anthropological perspective, indicating the degree of emotional intensity that was inherent in each of the levels of his cultural iceberg model. Hofstede et al. (2010) and Minkov et al. (2018) presented a view of societal dimensions from a sociological viewpoint. In the work of Bronfenbrenner (1979) and Bronfenbrenner and Morris (2006), a psychological view of child development as influenced by their environments is offered in their *Ecological Systems Theory*. This model provides a detailed, circular diagrammatic investigation of the ever-widening world of the child across five systems and how these interactions may shape the ways in which children develop and grow. Placing the child of any age and gender at the very centre of the investigation, the most immediate interactions and those with the most impact as experienced by the individual are with family, other children, perhaps church groups, neighbours, childcare and an even wider world of school. These interactions are the child's microsystem. The nature of these interactions and the ways in which children are treated and respond, as individuals, then influences the ways in which they respond to other children.

The next circle of impact is that of the interactions between the members of the microsystem. These could be between the child's teachers and the parents, between the child's neighbours or religious leaders and parents or between the child's peers and the parents. This is called the mesosystem and is, as can be seen, concerned with explaining the impact of the linkages and connections in the child's microsystem.

The next circle concerns actions that may not directly involve the child but which, nevertheless, affect the child's environment and have an indirect influence on their development. Identified as the exosystem, this type of interface examines the impact of two or more layers of the ecosystem, which may or may not include the child themselves. The impact of interactions that occur in the parents' workplaces, with extended family, with decisions made around parents' and neighbours' shared social lives, for example, are not usually within the sphere of interactions in which the child may directly be involved but nevertheless may have some significant consequences for the child and their relationships. Changes in routines at home that are made as the result of a parent being promoted or moving to another location for employment may readily change the pattern of interaction in the home. The macrosystem within which the other systems are embedded is constantly evolving from one generation to the other as it represents the wider, overarching cultural factors that influence the developing child. Contextual variables such as geographic location, social and economic status, religious observances, poverty and ethnicity are all broader influences that influence the ways in which children develop. These are important factors in child development as they combine in various ways to provide experiences for some children which are not present for others.

The final system is the chronosystem. This records and accounts for the patterns of environmental and transitional events that occur over the lifetime of the child. It is in this system that many of the traumatic and fearful experiences of refugee and asylum-seeker children can be located. The events and circumstances of forced migration for themselves and their families, in addition to the exposure to violence and cruelty as inflicted on themselves, their family members or members of their communities, may be exhibited in various behaviours when the children are newly arrived at schools in their new homelands. But, as with other changing historical and social occurrences, Bronfenbrenner's model acknowledges the possible ongoing impact of these for child development, while recognising that new patterns of interactions and experiences at any life stage have the potential to stabilise the pattern of interactions and mediate ongoing negative consequences. Chiu et al. (2016) investigated students' perceptions and expectations of school belonging across multiple diverse cultures using the macro level of Bronfenbrenner's *Ecological Systems Theory*. They found that the two aspects of cultural difference that proved to be the most significant in determining students' sense of belonging at school were sociological factors. These were Hofstede's dimensions of *Power Distance* and *Individualistic or Collectivist* cultures.

### Research findings

Our participants recognised and were sensitive to the microsystems at play in the lives of their students. Of note were the observations of a primary school principal in England and a secondary principal in New Zealand.

> Context: We have about 700 students, approximately. We have 90 per year group all the way from Reception up into Year 6. We're quite a big school. We serve a diverse community, and we do a lot of work with our community. They're very supportive. We're in a suburban leafy-type area but we've also got a block of high-rise flats. Since we were ranked as Outstanding by Ofsted, our demographics have changed a lot. We've got a lot of affluent parents that are moving in and want to bring their children but also, we have children who are socioeconomically deprived, who perhaps don't have so much. Overall, we serve a very diverse community; we've got 54 different languages in our school.

> *With this particular child that I'm talking about, because he came with the refugee status and his parents didn't speak any English at all, it was interesting because they made friends with another family in our school and they got close to them. This*

*meant we were able to tap into that other mom, who does speak English. They are a little bit more affluent in their status as well. She actually shared with us that this family has had a terrible experience, that they've been in Europe for quite a long time. This child didn't have any routines or base because they were just running around wherever they were placed. And he'd also experienced some emotional trauma – his older brother had passed away. So, although he's very happy in our school, we know there's a lot of underlying issues.*

Context: Around 1,400 students from Years 9 to 13 (ages 13 to 18). Our school is very diverse, and we received our first refugee students roughly 13 years ago.

*Those meals which we had hoped would provide a link between the community and school, we had been attending for quite a number of years, but when people stopped coming and it's like, "Why is that?". But I think it's because now we've got the siblings coming and the families do have a strong relationship with the school and they feel very confident and comfortable to come into the school – so perhaps the meals aren't as needed. I think, it is also… some of them I've noticed a pattern after two or three or four years in New Zealand, it's almost like they now are settled in New Zealand and sometimes that's when the trauma or the behavioural issues or dynamics of family issues start to come up. We have had a lot of families where that's been the case. At that point also valuing the family bringing the whole family, and having wraparound meetings with translators and a supportive, "We were on your side" sort of in a way, not saying, "You're not following the rules and we're going to stand you down".*

### Unique contexts, global principles

Each of these principals offered a thoughtful vignette about recognising the long-term and far-reaching effects of trauma. Our primary principal from England went outside normal channels to gather information on one of her students with a refugee background. Her efforts uncovered a boy who didn't have routines, who had been displaced emotionally and geographically and who had experienced great loss within his immediate family. Without her team's efforts, this student might have garnered little attention from the principal, as he presented as happy and sociable at school. Our high school principal from New Zealand observed that many of her families with refugee and asylum-seeker backgrounds stopped attending communal school meals, a behaviour she keenly recognised as a sign of their acceptance of the school community rather than rejection. This principal is also dealing with trauma and crises that have remained below the surface for years in some cases. She has taken a positive and holistic approach with these families, bringing in counsellors and translators and ensuring that a clear message of support is evident. These principals offer a sophisticated understanding of the lives of their students and families with refugee and asylum-seeker backgrounds. They recognise the long-term effects of forced transition and trauma and are attuned to these effects in the behaviours of their students.

Principals who create welcoming and safe environments for children with refugee and asylum-seeker backgrounds understand this work is complex and extends far beyond the first days and weeks after a new student enters school. As families become settled, in some cases years after their arrival, the routines that bring structure to their lives also provide time to think about their past experiences and issues can come to the surface. Patterns and schedules can give an outward appearance of calm, but there are events so traumatic, as Bronfenbrenner (1979) asserts through his chronosystem, that they impact individuals forever. Just as important, students are part of family, school, church and community systems and this reality magnifies their exposure to others who have suffered and who are dealing with their own trauma. As our two principals demonstrate, it is imperative to continually work to understand the experiences of these families and to recognise that cultures have very different ways of dealing with trauma, loss and sadness.

## Chapter conclusion

Students with refugee and asylum-seeking backgrounds bring both unique and exciting culture, language and values to their new schools and a host of challenges emanating from unimaginable loss, forced relocation and trauma. It is the responsibility of proactive principals and their staff members to work to understand, recognise and value the differences and experiences these individuals bring. It is also impingent upon school leaders to help newly arrived families recognise what is accepted and expected in the host school community. School personnel need to understand that the world views and experiences of their new arrivals will be vastly different than those of the host country. The convergence of these realities can lead to dynamic growth opportunities for everyone or major stress points as worlds collide. The reflective principal and staff must take it upon themselves to investigate what they do not understand; they must ask questions and seek outside information and experts. The more principals reflect and understand about their newly arrived families, the more likely they are to behave in supportive ways that create opportunities for growth across all constituents in the school. In Chapter 4, the deleterious effects of trauma and the importance of understanding and responding to it are discussed.

## References

Bronfenbrenner, U. (1979). *The Ecology of Human Development: Experiments by Nature and Design.* Harvard University Press.

Bronfenbrenner, U., & Morris, P. (2006). The bioecological model of human development. In W. Damon & R. Lerner (Eds.), *Handbook of Child Psychology: Theoretical Models of Human Development* (pp. 793–828). Wiley.

Chiu, M., Chow, B., McBride, C., & Mol, S. (2016). Students' sense of belonging at school in 41 countries: Cross-cultural variability. *Journal of Cross-Cultural Psychology*, 47(2), 175–196.

Hall, E. (1976). *Beyond Culture*. Knopf Doubleday Publishing Group.

Hargraves, V. (2019). *How to avoid a tokenistic or 'tourist' approach to diversity*. https://theeduca tionhub.org.nz/how-to-avoid-a-tokenistic-or-tourism-approach-to-diversity/.

Hofstede, G. (2001). *Culture's Consequences: Comparing Values, Behaviors, Institutions and Organizations Across Nations* (2nd ed.). Sage.

Hofstede, G., Hofstede, G. J., & Minkov, M. (2010). *Cultures and Organisations: Software of the Mind*. McGraw-Hill.

Minkov, M., Bond, M., Dutt, P., Schachner, M., Morales, O., Sanchez, C., … Mudd, B. (2018). A reconsideration of Hofstede's fifth dimension: New flexibility versus monumentalism data from 54 countries. *Cross-Cultural Research*, 53(3), 309–333.

Thier, M. (2013). Cultural awareness logs: A method for increasing international-mindedness among high school and middle school students. *The English Journal*, 102 (6), 46–53.

# 4   Trauma and loss

## Introduction

Creating places of welcoming and safety for children and families with refugee and asylum-seeker backgrounds is a difficult and important charge for all school leaders serving such individuals. Unlike other newly arrived families, these people have likely suffered forced displacement, loss of material wealth, years in refugee camps, loss of or separation from loved ones and the resulting trauma. This trauma is lasting, multi-faceted and pervasive; it is vital that school leaders understand how it manifests itself in the behaviours and emotions of children and families in the near-term and long after arriving in their host countries. With the voices of participants embedded throughout, this chapter describes the potential emotional, cognitive and intergenerational impacts of trauma and loss. Further, the chapter offers insights and observations from school leaders who are working to meet the needs of children and families with refugee and asylum-seeker backgrounds.

## Emotional impacts of trauma

Many students in schools who have refugee experiences and backgrounds are happy and well-adjusted to their new homelands and the cultural challenges and adventures that they offer. For many students, this is an authentic representation of their coping strategies, resilience and optimism. For other students with refugee and asylum-seeker experiences, the impact of the trauma that they have experienced is more apparent. All students with refugee and asylum-seeker experiences have suffered trauma. Displacement itself is a traumatic experience (Frater-Mathieson, 2004), which may have been added to by the circumstances of the forced migration, the journey to the new homeland and the resettlement conditions that they experience on arrival. It is important to understand the resiliencies and optimism that these students exhibit and acknowledge that they need supportive relationships at school and elsewhere (Losoncz, 2016; Uehling, 2015). It is equally critical to realise that not all students should be pathologised as mentally at risk, nor should it be assumed that the results of traumatic experiences should be immediately apparent or that

DOI: 10.4324/9781003090731-4

resettlement will instantly heal all effects of trauma and loss (Bryant-Davis, 2005a; Hart, 2009; Umer & Elliot, 2019). The impacts of loss and trauma may last a lifetime and only surface at various, different periods of the lives or may be regularly presented as mood swings, anxiety, fear and irrational behaviours (Frater-Mathieson, 2004; Lau et al., 2018; E. Stewart & Mulvey, 2013). In some circumstances there are contextual or cultural circumstances that are usually described as neglect, as the result of exposure to 'witnessing domestic violence, poor nutrition, poverty, and lack of educational opportunities' (De Bellis, 2005 p. 150). Teachers and others are required to help students negotiate both cultures to minimise additional stress and trauma as they settle into their new homeland expectations and customs (Doná & Berry, 1994).

Childhood and adolescent trauma, described as developmental trauma, and its impact, is an important aspect of attempting to understand the situation of these students. De Bellis (2010) describes five major ways in which the brain and body respond to an infinite number of stressors. These include impaired capacity for relationships, which De Bellis, (2010, p. 391) describes as a tendency for 'dysfunctional and traumatised' interactions with friends, family and the wider society to which they belong, which tend to cause more stressful and disturbing memories. A second impact may include distrust and a lack of confidence for those in authority, which can cause major problems for principals and teachers. There are a number of studies which discuss managing classroom behaviours of traumatised students with refugee and asylum-seeker experiences (see, for example Hue & Kennedy, 2013; Hyde et. al., 2011; Rutter & Jones, 1998). What is important to understand is that restoring trust can be difficult and the impact of the stressors that created the trauma are more detrimental as developmental trauma than they are as adult trauma. This is because in childhood they are believed to change biological stress symptoms and negatively impact on brain development. Experiencing intense fear or anxiety causes chemicals to rush to the brain causing tachycardia, hypertension, increased metabolic rate, hypervigilance, and increased levels of stress chemicals, including catecholamine.

### Research findings

Our leaders offered powerful insights on the effects of trauma on their students. Notable were vignettes from an Australian primary principal and an Australian high school principal.

> Context: I work at a K-6 school in a regional town with roughly 250 students. I've been a high school teacher, a high school principal, a primary school principal, and I also taught maths in high school, so I have a bit of an eclectic background. I've been here now for a while and have been one of the most stable principals; I've been here 11 years. Unfortunately, I do experience high staff turnover. We also have a high turnover of students. Over time, we probably always had refugee kids but not in high numbers.

Suddenly we were hit with a whole lot coming from Syria, and that was interesting.

*My real concern was around the trauma that we kept hearing from the children, that we needed to consider... the students asked me, "Do we have war in Australia?", and I'm very, you know, dramatic in replying, "No. We don't have war in Australia. We don't want it." And then one of the little fellows, he translated what I'd said to some of the other kids and all of a sudden there was a celebration. They are celebrating that we don't have war here, that we don't want it here and you're safe. And that was a couple of real moments for me with the kids, that the kids just want to be safe. We got a couple of kids who have a lot of trauma; one little girl, she lost all her siblings. She lost three siblings in a bombing, and she's also blind as a result of that. One day there was a big noise under the covered outdoor learning area, and she hit the deck as a response.*

Context: We are a high school (Years 7–12) in a capital city and I have been the principal for two years. We have 80% of our students from a non-English speaking background. We also have an Intensive English centre, which comprises refugees, international students and new arrivals. So that's part of our 80%. Many of our students come to us with extreme trauma, from Syria, Afghanistan, Iraq, and we have lots of students also from China. They come to our school initially to learn English in the Intensive English centre, but many of them stay with us because we run so many programs that support students from non-English speaking backgrounds.

*I just also want to mention, in the past, there's been a significant amount of trauma with our students. So, coming from the war-torn countries and the significant trauma that they've been through, the kids need additional support in terms of their well-being, their mental health, but also finances, ensuring that they've got the uniform or the basic supplies to come to school, the resources. The process has been pretty much — we started with helping the students to make sure that they could be in an education setting with the uniform and the books, and now it's turned into supporting staff with ensuring that they're all understanding the trauma that these students have faced.*

### Unique contexts, global principles

Each of our principals is keenly aware of the negative effects of trauma on their students and they have purposefully worked to create environments and policies to mitigate some of those effects. When our primary principal reported to her students that Australia has no domestic wars, they celebrated because they felt safe and because they have clearly experienced wars and great trauma and loss. Importantly, the students also celebrated because this principal has developed a trusting relationship with them and they believed her. The little girl who dived to the ground did so automatically as her experiences of horrific trauma and unimaginable loss have shaped how she interacts with her world. The Australian high school principal welcomes many students who may have experienced trauma at a much later age. This principal ensures these children have the basics including uniforms, books and supplies, so they come to school as regular students with regular things. This principal has used her work around supplying the basic school necessities as a springboard for conversation and education with her staff. Each of these principals spoke with great passion about the need to use the opportunities, tools and resources at their disposal to lessen the implications of trauma on their students.

Creating school environments where all students, particularly those who have suffered great trauma, feel safe and a part of the culture is the first order of business for principals. To begin, school personnel must acknowledge the scars and trauma their students have experienced, and it needs to be widely understood that while the effects of trauma may not be visible, they are pervasive. A schoolwide commitment is key to support these students, to affirm them and to build an environment of trust. Developing this commitment requires a comprehensive approach to educating each staff member about the impacts of trauma and the ways in which they can respond. This education also needs to account for the effects of trauma experienced by children of different ages. As the Australian high school principal and her staff illustrate, providing school necessities is an important step to supporting students with refugee and asylum-seeker experiences, but the power of such efforts is in their ability to unite staff around a central purpose. Principals have a unique vantage point from which they can leverage their authority, develop a caring vision and empower staff to respond to the comprehensive needs of their students.

## Cognitive impacts of trauma

Without an emotionally positive and optimistic emotional perspective, it is extremely difficult to engage optimally in cognitive tasks. Emotional and cognitive development are intrinsically intertwined in the development and activities of the brain. In addition to the emotional impacts of prolonged stressors as the result of trauma and loss, there is the possibility that areas of the brain associated with cognitive skills can be damaged or not allowed to develop naturally, resulting in increased chances of psychopathology (De Bellis, 2005, 2010). The fourth principle of development stressors indicates the need to consider a number of variables. Individual differences and environmental factors become important considerations in determining the possibility for healing and recovery, as do the type and frequency of the stressors, the timing of the incidences in relation to the developmental stage and brain maturation. De Bellis writes:

> Birth to adulthood is marked by progressive physical, behavioural, cognitive and emotional development, with changes in brain maturation paralleling these stages. Biological stress response systems are interconnected at

many levels to coordinate an individual's responses and adaptations to acute and chronic environmental stressors, and these interconnections influence brain development. In the developing brain, elevated levels of catecholamine and cortisol may lead to adverse brain development through a variety of mechanisms... As puberty begins, white cortical matter is maturing particularly in the prefrontal areas of the brain which house executive functions, planning, moral decisions and problem-solving. Subcortical areas of the brain linked to emotion, including amygdala, are also nearing maturity. As connections of inhibitory neurons from prefrontal areas to the amygdala mature, the ability to control thoughts and impulses develops.

(De Bellis, 2005, pp. 394–395)

In healthy development, these processes allow individuals to form a strong sense of identity, to understand the motivations and actions of others and develop abstract thinking. The executive functioning skills to which De Bellis refers include the cognitive capacities that are generally associated with 'good' classroom and school behaviours (MacLure et al., 2012). These include competencies in getting organised, initiating tasks, seeking feedback when required, inhibiting responses, managing emotions (self-regulation) and engaging positively. Importantly, executive function skills also include the ability to readily develop and access working memory and think flexibly around content knowledge and skills when faced with novel tasks. They also include a capacity to follow through and complete tasks, even in the face of other distractions, confirming their inclusion of motivational factors and capabilities (Meltzer, 2007; Meltzer et al., 2007; Moran & Gardner, 2007; Sellars, 2006, 2012).

It is easy to see how De Bellis' medical explanation and its implications for teaching and learning are important for educators, especially principals as they seek to integrate students with refugee and asylum-seeker experiences into their school communities. For individuals impacted by ongoing stressors, the onset of adolescence may cause a resurgence of behaviours associated with the trauma. These may include intense anger, inappropriate and unacceptable behaviours at school and in the classroom, a desire for revenge and, in extreme cases, thoughts of suicide. Jasnow and Ressler (2010) discuss the importance of taking into consideration the impact of personal conflict in interpersonal relationships, indicating that it is one of the 'most pervasive forms of stress... experienced by humans' (Jasnow & Ressler, 2010, p. 456). Unsurprisingly, they found that friendships and strong social support could mediate the impact of adult psychopathology, despite childhood experiences of trauma and interpersonal violence, providing school communities with additional incentives to include the families and communities of their students with refugee experiences in the social school networks and activities.

### Research findings

The effects of trauma on the cognitive development of children with refugee and asylum-seeker experiences was of paramount importance for our principals.

Particularly important observations were offered by two high school principals in the United States.

Context: We are not recognised as a separate school, but we are a program under the English as a Second Language department. We have a cap on students, and the number is quite small. I am in my third year as an administrator here. Prior to that, I was a language arts and English as an Additional Language/Dialect teacher. I have taught K-12, but most of my experience was at the middle school level as a teacher and as an instructional coach specialising in working with teachers who have English learners at the high school level. The demographic of our program has changed over the years, but we currently have a large Spanish-speaking population.

*For some of our students, they really see the growth in English; however, developing language is an individual, unique experience. Some of our students take longer than others, but we have had many families say that they appreciate the language that has been developed over the course of the year. Whereas with other students, we have a family saying, "No, they are not learning enough. They need to learn more English." It is just, I do not know, language development is a tricky thing and then you put a teenager into it, and then you put in all other kinds of things into it: trauma and just survival in a new country. So, there are other things that affect or impact how quickly you learn the language.*

Context: I am the proud principal of a high school (Grades 9–11) where most of our students come from Spanish-speaking backgrounds. Over 60% of our students have been in the country for two years or less. Our school is 100% composed of English-language learners. So, we've created this environment where we have thought about mastery-based learning with the English-language learner in mind. Although, my school just finished our fifth year of existence, so we're pretty much still in our infancy stages.

*When they first come to us, our intake process is, we ask our families all of those questions around: What has it been like? How long have you been in the country? So, we really get them invested in understanding that we're not just about academics, but about the whole child... We know that our population has experienced trauma more so than a traditional schooling population, so we included student support every day at 1 o'clock after the school day is officially over. We are heavily invested in our human resources, so we have two counsellors, two social workers, a pupil personnel worker, a parent engagement person. We're very heavily packed in our student support office, because we know that our kids need so much more than just teachers... A lot of just social-emotional support for our kids, in the beginning we only did one class per day, so those sorts of things. Because we know that once you turn the world upside down, you're going to have different expectations at home.*

### Unique contexts, global principles

Each of our principals offered insight about setting priorities for students and families with refugee and asylum-seeker backgrounds. Though academic development of students may be their school's primary mission, these principals are cognisant that learning will be mostly ineffective if students' wellbeing is not addressed. Our American leader who runs a small school within a school articulates the difficulty of learning English for older students and the reality that many families see English acquisition as indicative of their child's success in school. Further, this leader recognises the compounding effects of trauma, adolescence and transition on language development, a process that is incredibly varied among students in the best-case scenarios. Our second American high school principal, who leads a very large school, takes a direct and educative approach with parents from the point of intake, framing the role of schooling as being about more than academics. This principal has allocated significant funding to create a rich network of social-emotional supports for his students and he has reworked his school's entire schedule to enable students to benefit from those supports. Each of our principals observed that families have diverse expectations and aspirations for their students and this is no different for children who arrive with experiences of great trauma.

Navigating high school and the challenges of adolescence can be difficult for students who have matriculated through primary schools in the same system. But, for students with refugee and asylum-seeker backgrounds who have experienced trauma and are new to the conventions of western education, the challenge can be immense. The deleterious effects of trauma on language acquisition, concentration, behaviour, impulse control and a host of other variables is well documented. Our two principals highlight the importance of recognising trauma and putting wellbeing first. Importantly, our principals also make it a point to educate staff members and parents about the varied effects of trauma on student behaviour and achievement. By educating all stakeholders and building a school network rich with social supports as affirmed by Jasnow and Ressler (2010), principals can help to mitigate the effects of trauma. Still, school leaders must understand that prioritising the wellbeing of their students may be perceived as lowering academic rigour and expectations by some families who see education as a panacea to the inequities and horrors that have dominated their lives. As with all families, shared experiences do not translate into shared aspirations.

## Intergenerational trauma

Students with refugee and asylum-seeker experiences may express the impact of these experiences as poor concentration and hypervigilance among other behaviours (Blackwell & Melzak, 2000; Ehntholt et al., 2005). The behaviours exhibited by these students may be escalated or exacerbated by the quality of their interpersonal relationships with their parents or carers. The development of a sense of identity is not only dependent on healthy brain development as discussed but on positive personal relationships, especially with those who are close to them (Bryant-Davis, 2005a, 2005b; Jasnow & Ressler, 2010; Lau et al., 2018). The quality of these relationships depends, in the case of these students, on the capacities of the parents to overcome their own hurt and suffering as the result of their traumatic experiences of displacement, of the horrors of war, of loss and of the circumstances and the degree to which they are received in their new homelands. Many families and communities who survive the initial traumas of displacement and its circumstances are subjected to ongoing stress and anxieties in their places of resettlement. Children and young people are sensitive to and highly influenced by the levels of stress experienced by their parents and caregivers (see, for example J. Stewart, 2011, pp. 105–108). Known as intergenerational trauma or intergenerational transmission of trauma, distress can literally be transferred by one generation to another.

> Posttraumatic Stress Disorder (PTSD) and commonly comorbid psycho-pathology associated with the intergenerational transmission of violent trauma (i.e. dissociative, somatoform, affective, personality and substance use disorders) are serious public health problems... However, the specific mechanisms by which... are transmitted remain largely unknown.
>
> (Schechter, 2010, p. 256)

Posttraumatic Stress Disorder is the fifth and final way in which the body and brain react to extreme stressors. This disorder can frequently be found in students with refugee and asylum-seeker experiences. In addition to their own developmental trauma that they had experienced first-hand, many of these students indirectly witness the declining mental and, at times, physical health of their parents and caregivers as it is reflected in the deterioration of the standards of care and parenting that they had previously received (Bornstein, 2010; Hamilton & Moore, 2006; J. Stewart, 2011). In many cases where these situations exist, children and young people undergo an 'adultisation' and respond by taking on the responsibilities of the adult in the family unit, become unofficial carers for those who would normally care for them and lose their childlike characteristics and perspectives.

Perhaps one of the most confronting, cautionary examples of research is recorded by J. Stewart (2011). Engaging with support systems that were established to support students arriving in Canada from the African subcontinent as refugee students, she initially had some doubts about their need of the support as they appeared to be functioning extremely successfully in their adopted homeland and educational systems. Considering that they may have such high degrees of resilience and endurance as to render them immune from the impacts of trauma, she found, in interviewing them, that they had suffered horrific and sustained abuse that they had previously not revealed to anyone. Their stress symptoms, indicators of PTSD and unresolved grief, were all hidden under the behaviours of normality that they adopted. They had deep psychological issues and concerns, especially for their mothers who had endured brutal suffering and were now attempting to make new lives as single parents to their families. They were in perilous mental health. In this group of students, the signs of developmental trauma did not appear, in some cases, until two years after they were interviewed. This situation alone serves to alert principals and teachers to the multiple 'coping and covering up' strategies that some students employ to ease their distress and trauma. Student differences and diversity are multiple and multi-faceted, creating an ongoing responsibility for principals and teachers to remain sensitive and alert to indications that their students have suffered developmental trauma, PTSD or intergenerational trauma. The signals may be in attitudes, behaviours, cognitive challenges or simple signs of neglect. While inclusion and positive relationships are vital for the wellbeing of these students, it is important to be cognisant of the times when those may not be enough.

### Research findings

Nearly all the principals we interviewed talked about the effects of trauma on entire families and the repercussions of this intergenerational trauma on students. Two principals who shared particularly relevant observations were a primary principal in Northern Ireland and a primary principal in Australia.

> Context: Our school (Reception to Year 7) has been open since the beginning of the twentieth century and it was opened to serve the local population at the time, but over the years we've now started to serve a population that is a little bit different. I would say off the top of my head we have about 30% newcomer children at the moment; we have probably two out of every six children that are asylum seekers. We began to get Chinese children in 2004, and it was at the end of 2010 we got our first Somali child. He had never been in school before; we also had no idea what to do with the boy we saw. We had no idea about refugees, or asylum seekers. It's been a process, it has evolved over the last 10 years and I know that it will continue to evolve as the staff come on board.

> *We're working towards being recognised as a nurturing school at the moment. We're also working towards a Nurturing Award. For me, it's all about encouragement and about understanding the Adverse Childhood Experiences that many of our children have come through. We have heard some terrible stories and those families are so wonderful, so resilient and so sanguine about what they have come through. Many of the Somali families actually say, "this is in the past, we're fine." For me, it's understanding some of what they've been through – even if they don't tell you – and then making that nurturing connection with the children first.*

> Context: I have taught in high schools and was a behaviour consultant prior to becoming a principal. Our school is kindergarten to Grade 6 and is

in a regional centre. We have around 150 students, with about 15% students from a culturally linguistically diverse background. We try to have a diverse staff to match the diverse needs of our students; I have one lady and she was a refugee herself and speaks the language of some of our students.

*For some children when they first come, they've actually never sat on the toilet. Because that's not a cultural thing, to sit on the toilet. There's so many little, tiny things that people don't think about… so we try to help children to navigate walking between two worlds, because effectively that's what they do. But, you've got parents who, over time, they've got that initial sense of safety, then they've got those feelings of guilt, then there's people still back home and they want to send money to them. They haven't been educated in terms of how to use money and what it means to have bills and all of those sorts of things. You've got people who have just been fighting for food in a refugee camp, which is a dangerous place. And then they come here and may have been separated from their children for the first time and sometimes the kids have actually been with their parents every single day of their lives, because they have been in a refugee camp with no school.*

### Unique contexts, global principles

Each of our principals were keenly aware of the behaviours and emotions of parents with refugee and asylum-seeker backgrounds. Our primary principal in Northern Ireland shared insight about working with Somali families who had endured horrific experiences. While the families present a façade of contentment and express a desire to move forward, this principal recognises that trauma can continue to harm families long after the source is removed. A reflective leader, this principal strives to understand her families and she gains their trust by first building nurturing relationships with their children. Our Australian principal also cautions about the façade of normalcy that may appear when families develop a sense of safety. His observation about the child and the toilet is illustrative of the massive leap that many parents take when bringing their families to new countries and cultures. This principal's caution about the depth of guilt that parents may feel for loved ones left behind and his observations that many parents may be anxious at being separated from their children are important. Both principals approach their families with refugee and asylum-seeker backgrounds with a desire to connect, to understand their lived experiences, and a recognition that the verbal and non-verbal messages they receive may not align with reality.

Principals who effectively meet the needs of their refugee and asylum-seeker students understand these children are shaped by their families and what happens at home. Parents may be depressed and feel guilty because they were not able to protect their own families, they left family members behind, or they had to fight for food or shelter for their families. Additionally, parents and grandparents may struggle much more than their young children to acclimatise to new cultures, modern living and conventions. Children are particularly aware of their parents' stress and highly protective of their families; this influences their own behaviour. These children may come to school with particular family-learned habits around food, money and even freedom. Principals need to recognise that all these complex relationships and interwoven variables are not a deficit, but rather a reality for these families. School leaders can work towards helping this complex reality by supporting the whole family. Developing nurturing programs, policies and practices which include children, parents and extended family members is an important step for any school community.

## Chapter conclusion

While it may seem obvious, the first order of business for principals working with children who have suffered great trauma is to create a safe and welcoming environment. To do this, principals need to educate their staff members about trauma and the experiences their newly arrived students have suffered. The entire staff must understand the causes of trauma, its effects and how to support students and families who have experienced it. Educators need to understand that trauma affects entire families, and, in some cases, students are going home to parents and other family members who are suffering greatly. In other cases, individuals may appear happy, adjusted and secure but this outward appearance contrasts with what they are experiencing internally. Trauma is hard to leave behind and its effects can emerge months or years after arriving in a host country. As the principals in this chapter suggest, schools need a whole-family approach that is welcoming, supporting, educative and long-lasting. Reflective principals must stay attuned to their students and recognise when behaviours change, and then work to understand why and what to do next. In Chapter 5, the imperative of wellbeing and belonging are explored.

## References

Blackwell, D., & Melzak, S. (2000). *Far from the Battle but Still at War: Troubled Refugee Children in School*. Child Psychotherapy Trust.
Bornstein, M. (2010). From measurement to meaning in caregiving and culture. In C. Worthman, P. Plotsky, D. Schechter, & C. Cummings (Eds.), *Formative Experiences: The Interaction of Caregiving, Culture and Developmental Psychobiology* (pp. 36–50). Cambridge University Press.
Bryant-Davis, T. (2005a). Afterword. In *Thriving in the Wake of Trauma* (pp. 173–181). Praeger.
Bryant-Davis, T. (2005b). Introduction. In *Thriving in the Wake of Trauma* (pp. 1–11). Praeger.
De Bellis, M. (2005). The psychobiology of neglect. *Child Maltreatment*, 10(2) 150–172. doi:10.1177/1077559505275116.
De Bellis, M. (2010). Developmental traumatology: A commentary on the factors for risk and resiliency in the case of an adolescent Javanese boy. In C. Worthman, P. Plotsky, D. Schechter, & C. Cummings (Eds.), *Formative Experiences: The Interaction of*

*Caring, Culture and Developmental Psychobiology* (pp. 390–397). Cambridge University Press.

Doná, G., & Berry, J. W. (1994). Acculturation attitudes and acculturative stress of Central American refugees. *International Journal of Psychology*, 29(1), 57–70.

Ehntholt, K., Smith, P., & Yule, W. (2005). School-based cognitive-behavioural therapy: Group intervention for refugee children who have experienced war-related trauma. *Clinical Child Psychology and Psychiatry*, 29(1), 57–70.

Frater-Mathieson, K. (2004). Refugee trauma, loss and grief: Implications for intervention. In R. Hamilton & D. Moore (Eds.), *Educational Interventions for Refugee Children* (pp. 12–34). Routledge.

Hamilton, R., & Moore, D. (2006). *Educational Interventions for Refugee Children*. Routledge.

Hart, R. (2009). Child refugees, trauma and education: Interactionist considerations on social and emotional needs and development. *Educational Psychology in Practice*, 25(4), 351–368. doi:10.1080/02667360903315172.

Hue, M.-T., & Kennedy, K. J. (2013). Building a connected classroom: Teachers' narratives about managing the cultural diversity of ethnic minority students in Hong Kong secondary schools. *Pastoral Care in Education*, 31(4), 292–308. doi:10.1080/02643944.2013.811697.

Hyde, M., Carpenter, L., & Conway, R. (Eds.). (2011). *Diversity and Inclusion in Australian Schools*. Oxford University Press.

Jasnow, A., & Ressler, K. (2010). Interpersonal violence as a mediator of stress-related disorders in humans. In C. Worthman, P. Plotsky, D. Schechter, & C. Cummings (Eds.), *Formative Experiences: The Interactions of Caregiving, Culture and Developmental Psychobiology* (pp. 451–462). Cambridge University Press.

Lau, W., Silove, D., Edwards, B., Forbes, D., Bryant, R., McFarlane, A., … O'Donnell, M. (2018). Adjustment of refugee children and adolescents in Australia: Outcomes from wave three of the Building a New Life in Australia study. *BMC Medicine*, 16(1), 157. doi:10.1186/s12916-018-1124-5.

Losoncz, I. (2016). Building safety around children in families from refugee backgrounds: Ensuring children's safety requires working in partnership with families and communities. *Child Abuse & Neglect*, 51, 416–426. doi:10.1016/j.chiabu.2015.09.001.

MacLure, M., Jones, L., Holmes, R., & MacRae, C. (2012). Becoming a problem: Behaviour and reputation in the early years classroom. *British Educational Research Journal*, 38(3), 447–471. doi:10.1080/01411926.2011.552709.

Meltzer, L. (2007). Executive function: Theoretical and conceptual frameworks. In L. Meltzer (Ed.), *Executive Function in Education: From Theory to Practice* (pp. 1–4). The Guildford Press.

Meltzer, L., Pollica, L., & Barzillai, M. (2007). Executive function in the classroom: Embedding strategy into everyday teaching practices. In L. Meltzer (Ed.), *Executive Function in Education: From Theory to Practice* (pp. 165–193). The Guildford Press.

Moran, S., & Gardner, H. (2007). Hill, skill and will: Executive function from a multiple intelligences perspective. In L. Meltzer (Ed.), *Understanding Executive Function* (pp. 19–38). Guildford.

Rutter, J., & Jones, C. (Eds.). (1998). *Refugee Education: Mapping the Field*. Stylus Publishing.

Schechter, D. (2010). Multigenerational ataques de nervios in a Dominician American family: A form of intergenerational transmission of violent trauma. In C. Worthman, P. Plotsky, D. Schechter, & C. Cummings (Eds.), *Formative Experiences: The Interaction* of *Caregiving, Culture and Developmental Psychobiology* (pp. 256–269). Cambridge University Press.

Sellars, M. (2006). The role of intrapersonal intelligence in self directed learning. *Issues in Educational Research*, 16(1), 95–119.

Sellars, M. (2012). Exploring executive function: Multiple Intelligences' personalised mapping for success. *International Journal of Learning*, 18(3), 293–304.

Stewart, E., & Mulvey, G. (2013). Seeking safety beyond refuge: The impact of immigration and citizenship policy upon refugees in the UK. *Journal of Ethnic and Migration Studies*, 40(7), 1023–1039. doi:10.1080/1369183x.2013.836960.

Stewart, J. (2011). *Supporting Refugee Children: Strategies for Educators*. University of Toronto Press.

Uehling, G. (2015). The responsibilization of refugees in the United States: On the political uses of psychology. *Anthropological Quarterly*, 88(4), 997–1028. www.jstor.org/stable/43955500?seq=1.

Umer, M., & Elliot, D. (2019). Being hopeful: Exploring the dynamics of post-traumatic growth and hope in refugees. *Journal of Refugee Studies*, 1–23. doi:10.1093/jrs/fez002.

# 5 Wellbeing and belonging

## Introduction

School leaders have an obligation to develop an environment where the adults know young people well and focus on student wellbeing as the highest priority. This is particularly true for students with refugee and asylum-seeker backgrounds, given the complex realities they have endured in their physical, psychological and emotional journeys to their new homes. Schools must be places where the whole community cares deeply about children's individual and collective journeys. Promoting wellbeing and providing students with a sense of belonging are vital requisites of a successful school and this chapter offers research and participant examples for enhancing school climate, culture and ethos, care and empathy.

## School climate, culture and ethos

The individual characteristics of schools have been investigated for over 100 years as they are recognised as reflecting the values and beliefs of the school leaders and as being an important aspect of school life (Cohen, 2006; Cohen et al., 2013). These characteristics are variously known as school climate, school culture and school ethos, depending on the particular aspect of the school that is the focus of the study. The initial investigations into school climate focused on the physical aspects of the school and its organisation, but subsequent studies have examined the potential for school climate to impact on students' mental health and wellbeing. Consequently, studies of school climate have expanded to examine the personal contributions of all members of the school community, including teachers', students' and parents' perceptions of the climate of the school. Field and Abelson (1982) summarised the existing literature some decades ago and developed a three-tier model of school climate. In this model they proposed that the impact of (i) the organisation level was mediated by the (ii) level of the group climate, which in turn was influenced by (iii) personal experiences of school climate, described as the psychological level. They identified the essence of school climate as the feelings of belonging and connectedness that individuals experienced in relation to the school. This view has been substantiated by more recent studies

DOI: 10.4324/9781003090731-5

(see, for example, Aldridge et al., 2016; Bradshaw et al., 2014; Cohen et al., 2009). School climate has been described as being 'shaped by the quality of the relationships between individuals at the school, the quality of the teaching and learning that takes place and the physical, social and emotional safety of the students' (Aldridge et al., 2016, p. 6).

Positive school climate is understood to be a more nuanced and subjective aspect of overall school culture and is currently considered to be an area of highest priority for student wellbeing, and more especially for the wellbeing of students with refugee and asylum-seeker experiences (Bradshaw et al., 2014; Loukas & Robinson, 2004; Walters, 2012). These students not only need a sense of belonging to a positive school climate but an awareness that they can make an important contribution to shaping and developing it. In order to achieve this, students with refugee and asylum-seeker experiences need to have positive relationships with peers and teachers and positive learning experiences that meet their academic needs.

School culture itself is a reflection of the principal's leadership mode and attitudes. Erikson (1987, p. 12) provided a definition of school culture which is still informative today. He stated that school culture 'is a system of ordinary, taken-for-granted meanings and symbols with both explicit and implicit content that is, deliberately and non-deliberately, learned and shared among members of a naturally bonded group'.

The problematic areas for students with refugee and asylum-seeker experiences who seek to become part of the school culture are multiple. Some revolve around the questions of unpacking the ordinary meanings and symbols, most especially those with implicit meanings but also those with explicit meanings in cultures and organisations that are hitherto unknown to them and at times may prove to be countercultural to their beliefs and understandings of school. Other questions interrogate the means by which these students can belong to 'the naturally bonded group' without losing a sense of identity with their heritage, language, customs and belief systems. School culture and school ethos are terms that are frequently used interchangeably in the literature as defining ethos has been considered to be problematic.

Solvason (2005) determined that *ethos* was a product of school culture, indicating that culture was tangible, and that ethos was a more nebulous construct. This distinction was supported by Glover and Coleman (2005) who concluded that school ethos is more difficult to measure than school climate or school culture, that it is a more general term and that it is more subjective in nature. Donnelly (2000) distinguished between the written, formal aspects of school ethos and the lived experiences of this documentary ethos as students in the classroom, indicating that a critical gap frequently exists between these two aspects of school ethos. Both of these are heavily value laden and a lack of congruence between what is articulated in policy and what students experience in school has the potential to complicate pathways to authentic school belonging for all students, but is most critical for students from refugee and asylum-seeker backgrounds who may find the disparities confusing and bewildering. The more closely the lived reality resembles that of the articulated foundational school values, the greater the potential for these students to find wellbeing and belonging at school.

### Research findings

Our participants shared insights on their lived experiences of school culture, climate and ethos. Notable were the observations of a high school principal in the eastern United States and a primary principal in New Zealand.

Context: Our school is 100% composed of English-language learners, with 85% of our seats reserved for students who attend the eighth grade in public schools and the other 15% of our seats are left open for students who are newly arrived in the country. Most of our students come from Spanish-speaking backgrounds, so most are from Guatemala, Honduras, El Salvador, and then we have a sprinkle of everything you can probably think of. Our Arabic population is growing, so a lot of students from Syria, Afghanistan, that population is growing and that's been more recent than our Latino population.

*What I'll say is, we've always been different. We have appreciated difference in a way that has allowed us to build a school culture where our kids feel that their difference is going to make the world better. The number one thing that we teach our kids is, you have to learn how to narrate your own story so that no one else narrates it for you. I think that taking kids on experiences like sharing their stories, their immigration stories, in front of hundreds of lawyers in New York or having one of our students speak at Harvard to a number of students there – those are the experiences that are really going to get them to understand the world that we live in, right? It's not about what happens within the four walls of our school building, for the most part. It's about the experiences that they have in the communities that they come from. I think that what we're teaching them are the skills to be able to navigate that world, and I think that's why we're so different.*

Context: I am principal of a school of around 750 students, both boys and girls, from Years 1 to 6. We are an exceptionally diverse school. At the beginning of this year, we had over 70 ethnicities represented at our school, so it really is a fantastic place. I have been a principal now for 13 years, and in education for around 24 years at a range of schools, both independent and public. This is my third principalship. And other than that, I haven't taught internationally, but have a reasonable amount of experience as part of the LEAP (Leading Educators Around the Planet) exchange to Canada, which was fantastic. I've also spoken internationally a number of times regarding our curriculum and teaching English. But obviously, my real passion is for teaching and learning.

> *One thing for teachers working with refugee families is a highly relational warm classroom environment where children are able to be emotionally regulated and feel safe and have a sense of belonging. That's one part itself in quite a complex piece... So it's also how the teacher goes about breaking down those obstacles, which is quite significant as well. For me, you really need to have that big quite special combination: of love; ability to create a lovely learning culture in your room; knowing your stuff in terms of your pedagogy, that is, knowing it from new entrant to a higher level; and, then be prepared to go the extra mile and connecting with your students.*

### Unique contexts, global principles

Despite their different contexts and student cohorts, these two principals have acknowledged the importance of school culture, its impact on student learning and its role in validating what their schools value and strive towards for their communities. The primary school principal from New Zealand has a strong focus on nurturing these younger students with strong positive relationships and classroom practices which provide emotionally safe classroom cultures in which students from refugee and asylum-seeker backgrounds can build their foundational academic and social skills. The high school principal from the US has very different student concerns and opportunities to consider when developing school culture. His school culture is heavily focused on student empowerment, identity formation and making positive contributions to society because of their differences, not in spite of them. Both principals have undertaken the same process of critically reflecting on what their leadership skills and capacities can bring to the school community and, because they recognise culture as an aspect of schooling, they can strongly influence their environments. They use their personal understandings, values and beliefs to develop schools which can enrich the learning journeys of students by providing the support and expectations of a like-minded community.

Cultures such as these do not just happen. Irrespective of the geographical location, the processes that determine school culture are the same. Principals must get to know their communities and their needs. They need to interrogate the school's policies and practices to evaluate their efficacy in relation to the needs of their students, their aspirations and their diversity. Continued collaboration with all the stakeholders (students, parents, teachers and other staff) provides opportunities for principals to be informed, to evaluate and to renew their dedication to cooperatively maintaining effective, positive school cultures. These cultures start at the school gate and permeate all the interactions that occur in the school context. School culture is not singularly established in the documents or policies of the school. As these two principals have articulated, their school cultures are evidenced in the activities and attitudes which are implemented as all the everyday activities and students' experiences within the learning community. School culture, including the unspoken, taken-for-granted knowledge and practices that comprise the hidden curriculum in all schools, is the mirror through which the values and beliefs of their principals can be observed.

# Care

Foundational to building school cultures that are inclusive of refugee and asylum-seeker students, is a capacity to care. Noddings' (2012) philosophy of care in schools requires no long, rational discourse to justify this construct, but instead posits that, as humans in the world, most individuals have a natural instinct to care, having experienced some degree of being cared for themselves. In terms of a philosophy from which to build a productive and inclusive teaching and learning context, the ethic of care presents powerful perspectives from which decisions are made, professional responsibilities and criteria are met, and overarching guidelines, policies and mandatory frameworks are interpreted and implemented. This ethic does not rely on principles and rules in its inter-actions, but instead focuses on discussion and consideration of the circumstances of the individuals involved in each situation, focusing on bringing about the best, most positive and caring solution in each context. Recognising that indi-viduals are unique, especially in the case of students with refugee and asylum-seeker experiences, so then are their concerns, situations and needs. An ethic of care demands responses and resolutions that demonstrate efforts to find strate-gies and responses that reflect genuine concern for each individual and their situation. In this manner, one of the features of moral education from the perspective of the ethic of care is *dialogue*.

This *dialogue* helps distinguish between the ethic of care and virtue ethics (Noddings, 2012). Virtue ethics refers to circumstances in which teachers may insist on practices and procedures that they believe are good for the students, but which are inappropriate or disliked by the students themselves. Students are at the centre of the discussion and response, seeking to find positive ways to overcome challenges according to the needs of those who are participating in caring relationships. Dialogue is important to moral education as it is the means through which teachers can get to know their students better, develop a com-monly understood framework and relationship within which to work and assess the efficacy of their caring. Dialogue also accommodates personal growth in which various perspectives can be examined, different ways of knowing and doing can be investigated, and students may learn to question factors that impact their own lives and values, dispositions and attitudes, a critical aspect of educating students with refugee and asylum-seeker experiences.

The role of the *cared for* – notably the students (but also other stakeholders) as individuals who participate and reciprocate in these caring interactions – is a vital component of this ethic. Caring individuals may be the most significant key to building school ethos. As students reciprocate as caring individuals, they are facilitated in the understanding and development of attitudes and disposi-tions that represent and produce positive and supportive contact and commu-nication with others. Not to be confused with the perspectives of moral education as presented by the cognitive developmentalists, Noddings (2012) discusses this component of moral education as *modelling*. A major focus of modelling is on the growth of the students, acting as both carers and cared for.

Supported and enabled by dialogue, caring behaviours are modelled, not just read about, discussed, or mandated. Teachers and other adults need to be committed to modelling what caring interactions *look like* when demonstrated daily in a variety of situations of diverse complexity. In this school, the caring is authentic and palpable. Caring originates in a personal space to which all adults are genuinely committed as a whole-school focus, on this philosophical perspective.

*Practice* is also a core component of moral education from the perspective of the ethic of care. In some educational contexts, this is interpreted as some type of community service, which may or may not help students develop their skills in caring for others. Curriculum and support practices must be implemented in ways that facilitate opportunities for students and adults to practise caring for each other on a continuous basis throughout schooling. Collaborative learning situations offer students multiple occasions to work with others, to support and encourage classmates and to develop positive caring dispositions. Caring schools seek out programs that support student development of sound positive interactions with diverse peers, and regularly implement strategies and tasks with the specific intention of supporting students' positive interactions with all others in the school.

*Confirmation* is a unique aspect of Noddings' ethic of care. This is the act of affirming the best in someone to help them grow in ways that they are striving for, in ways that they value, and in ways that are important to them. Confirming supports the notion of high expectations for all, in which every learner is considered capable of expanding their strengths, developing new knowledge and skills and being successful. For confirmation to be authentic, it must be valued by both the adults confirming the achievements and the students whose competencies are being valued. This can be facilitated by dialogue which enables teachers to know their students' goals and aspirations. In the action of confirming someone, it is important that the affirmation be intended to support the development of the students becoming the best person they could possibly be. The continuity of dialogue and caring interactions that permit trust to develop are an essential part of this process. Establishing, developing and maintaining caring relationships that empower true confirmation take time.

### Research findings

Our participants shared insights on their lived experiences of creating a culture of care. Notable were the observations of a primary school principal in the United States and a primary principal in Australia.

> Context: I know I'm the most diverse school in the county in terms of elementary schools. We're probably one of the most diverse schools in the state. Currently, I have 30 countries and 26 languages represented. The school has just over 1,000 students, 100% of students qualify for free and reduced lunch and around 650 students are English Speakers of other

Languages (ESOL). So, the largest population are my Hispanic, my Spanish-speaking students but after that, it will be my students from the Middle East speaking Pashto, Farsi, those students from Iraq, Afghanistan, Pakistan, and then from different countries in Africa.

*It is keeping me up at night because I went to a seminar recently at the beginning of COVID and the presenter said, "The worst thing you can do right now is lose connection with your staff and students." Like, the academics we can work on, but if you lose that connection with the school, it's going to be so hard to get that connection back. So, I'm constantly thinking of ways to keep the connection, from cooking classes to comedians for the staff, like I've thought of just anything, I've gone to their homes and dropped off gifts to every single person on my staff or to see if he's gotten that Amazon gift from me, or something to say, "I appreciate you and stay connected, from…" I'm just trying to think of ways to let them know that I'm here. The other administrators are here to support them.*

Context: The school has about 250 students and roughly 20% identify as Aboriginal. Only around 50% of the students in Year 6 started in kindergarten and there is a high mobility rate of students annually. We're characterised by poverty and family dysfunction. I have had more than 90% of my students on personalised learning plans. Unfortunately, I do experience high staff turnover now and then for pregnancies, retirements, the Bible schools. We probably always had refugee kids but not in high numbers. We were sort of suddenly hit with a whole lot coming from Syria, and that was interesting.

*I just have one major criteria for all of my staff and that is I expect them to be kind. It's just a simple thing, I know, and it's just be kind to everyone; we have lots of students and all sorts of trauma backgrounds. How hard is it just to stop and listen and take a moment? And that's the quality that I look for in all my staff, that they have a kindness about them, a genuine interest in it. That's what I look for outright, and we worked really hard here. Second thing, it's important to be interested. I don't know that we have to be all-encompassing and aware of every culture, aware of every religion. But I think you have to be respectful. I think you have to understand what respect looks like; you have to be a willing learner.*

### Unique contexts, global principles

Half a world apart, these principals each recognise the vital importance of caring for others, its effect on staff morale and its power to make people feel valued and a part of something bigger. The primary principal from the United States has made overt support and concern for her staff a centre piece of her practice. The Covid-19 pandemic, which has taken a terrible toll on her school community, has only caused her to lean into that work. Her continual efforts to show her staff and students they are valued certainly go beyond most principal job descriptions, but it is evident that her notion of care is foundational to her approach. The primary principal from Australia is faced with many of the same challenges highlighted by her American counterpart. With high rates of student mobility, much diversity, great poverty and challenging home situations, this principal has explicitly sought out caring teachers as her first and most important priority for developing an environment that values every child. And, with a 'moral purpose' to educate every student, this principal has a powerful understanding of care being about both belonging and betterment. Each of these principals practise an ethic of care that is part of their leadership DNA and has been refined by years of working with vulnerable populations seeking belonging. These leaders model what they seek in the educators with whom they surround themselves.

Principals, by virtue of their chosen profession, undoubtedly have a deeply ingrained ethic of care. But, to give this ethic of care a purpose, to use it to develop a better school for all stakeholders, requires action. Working in collaboration with their communities, principals need to evaluate their policies and the ways they make decisions about supporting students and families. Approaches based on a one-size-fits-all mentality have little space in a caring community that values the individual. Principals must demonstrate care for their staff members from their hiring practices to ongoing acknowledgement. Principals must also see that care is taught and nurtured in classrooms where students are engaged in acts of care for themselves, their peers, their community and the planet. As these two principals exemplify and as is evidenced in their schools, an ethic of care is rooted in a genuine interest in their students, their staff members and their community. These principals care purposefully because they understand it is the most powerful part of offering belonging and developing a culture that promotes caring acts. Principals are indeed caring people, but it is the wellbeing of teachers and students that acts as a barometer to how effectively that care is being actioned.

## Empathy

Empathy is a human emotion that can be powerful in the context of building meaningful relationships critical to wellbeing of students with refugee and asylum-seeker backgrounds and considered necessary for humanity (Ford, 2014; Gutstein & Peterson, 2005; Mirra, 2018). However, there are multiple views about the nature and types of empathy, in addition to what elicits an emphatic response. Davis (1983) discussed empathy as a complex construct, indicating that his four-dimension scale increasingly lends itself to a multidimensional approach. He lists *perspective taking* as an indication of better social functioning, *fantasy* as a psychologically emotional response, *empathic concern* as feelings of sympathy and concern for others and *personal distress*, which he describes as feelings of anxiety and discomfort in emotionally charged social situations. Eliciting any of these emphatic responses means engaging in relationship building. However, in some contexts there is little time or encouragement for teachers to develop these relationships (see, for example, Ferfolja, 2009; Ferfolja & Vickers,

2010; Ferfolja et al., 2018). Additionally, empathy is not the same for everyone. It is subject, as are many emotions, to attitudes and values, personal beliefs and cultural norms. Nussbaum (2001) in discussing the related emotion of compassion determined that there are three cognitive judgements that are made to elicit a compassionate response: a judgement of the 'size' of the suffering and if it is considered to be serious; an appraisal of the suffering – that the individual did not deserve to suffer, or to suffer to the degree that they have; and the extent to which the compassionate individuals can envisage themselves in the same situation. She also provides an important reminder that social and moral judgements about compassion need to be made with an understanding of the temporary nature of the suffering which is related to specific circumstances and that these individuals who elicit compassion still have agency. In the case of students and families with refugee and asylum-seeker experiences, their capacities for agency may be swiftly diminished in the face of increased regulations, changing policies and educational documentation and procedures.and educational documentation and procedures.

Mirra (2018) notes that empathy itself is politicised and inequitable in its distribution. She offers a critical understanding of empathy and discusses strategies to be implemented in schools to promote the development of empathy as two separate but related entities: personal empathy and *Critical Civic Empathy*. Positing that individual, personal empathy for individuals is valuable, she asserts that it can lead to a lack of awareness of this politicalising and inequity due to the social and cultural factors that invariably impact on an individual's capacity for empathy for specific, other individuals. She suggests that the study of *Critical Civic Empathy* should be the foundation of all work in education and provides a model for study, based on three principles. She illustrates these by providing curriculum opportunities in which engagement with the model and these principles are readily encountered across diverse syllabus domains.

- It begins from an analysis of the social positions, power and privilege of all parties involved;
- It focuses on the ways that personal experiences matter in public life;
- It fosters democratic dialogue and civic action committed to equity and justice.(Mirra, 2018, p. 7)

The four-square typography of empathy in her *Typology of Empathy* model (p. 11) includes *humanisation* based on the Freirean notion (Freire, 1970); a square for how those predisposed to this perspective may take action as a result of their commitment to humanity; an opposite square for *imaginative refusal*, which emphasises the importance of recognising and investigating the type of rhetoric that is frequently populated in the media and in national and other policies regarding refugee and asylum-seeker populations; and finally, a square for *false empathy*, which is often found in public arenas by politicians seeking to gain public kudos but which, in fact, is insincere. These latter statements are couched in terms of '*we*' and use the context of 'national' views and values, and are, on closer examination, politically manipulative and culturally divisive.

Other views of empathy come from cognitive science (Marsh, 2012), psychiatry (Koss-Chioino, 2006), phenomenological philosophy (Ratcliffe, 2012) and even from combining engineering and peace studies (Hopple & Choi-Fitzpatrick, 2017). Arguably the most useful understanding of radical empathy comes from Ratcliffe (2012, p. 477). Acknowledging that the experiences of one individual are interpreted by others in the context of a shared world experience, he posits that, in some cases, where the experiences cannot be construed as part of a shared understanding of the world, then it is necessary to temporarily 'suspend' what is taken for granted, what is personally understood about society and culture, and to develop a new frame of reference in order to deeply understand the experiences of others and empathise. Indicating that cultural difference may make empathy more difficult, Ratcliffe also points to the importance of examining the content of the other's experiences, echoing Nussbaum's (2001) cognitive judgements that relate to compassion-eliciting experiences. However, in order to elicit authentic, radical empathy, other types of empathy (mundane empathy) must be recognised and resisted. He states:

> All instances of radical empathy are united by a qualitative difference from mundane empathy—their recognition of a variable sense of belonging to a shared world, something that is more usually overlooked.
>
> (Ratcliffe, 2012, p. 479)

The empathy that Ratcliffe (2012) dismisses as 'mundane' are three regular types of empathy: cognitive empathy, where there is sufficient shared knowledge to understand the hurt, but not necessarily to do anything to ease it; emotional empathy, which describes the feeling that one individual may literally pass to another so that the 'other' may take on the feelings of those suffering; and compassionate empathy, which is compassion felt for those who suffer and that prompts action to support and help. However, the notion of compassionate empathy with its tradition of action is historically associated with gifting – a practice which is associated with personal satisfaction for the giver and consequently does not solely benefit the individuals with whom they empathise (Lampert, 2006). While Ratcliffe concedes that all types of empathy involve being open to others, he concludes that radical empathy is set apart from that which involves sharing a world, and in that way enables accessing the experiences of others that may otherwise prove to be elusive. Radical empathy requires deliberate focus and practice. It requires losing all the regular frames of reference that help explain experiences in a shared world. What is revealed is a deeper understanding of the experiences of others. In the context of schools and education, this thinking may not seem to be particularly useful or relevant, but what it does help illustrate is that, irrespective of the depth of compassionate empathy that is felt for students with refugee and asylum-seeker experiences and their communities, and the actions that are taken to help develop a sense of wellness and belonging, there are deeper layers of experiences of suffering that only those who engage in this phenomenological perspective of radical empathy can begin to understand.

### Research findings

Our participants offered deeply insightful perspectives on empathy. Notable were the observations of a primary school principal in Australia and a secondary principal in Australia.

> Context: A small K-6 educational and community hub in the inner city with around 150 students. There was about three and a half years where every new-arrival student of primary school age that moved to this city started in that school. We had up to 45% refugee students, who were newly arrived, at any one point in time. I had teachers who have masters who grew up in Kenya, who also speak Swahili; that was really, really helpful. I have one lady at the moment... and she was a refugee herself from Afghanistan and she speaks the language of the students.

> *I imagine the old duck image, calm on the surface of the water with its little legs going underneath. But it gets deeper, because you have to control all your little micro behaviours and your fingers and everything else like that. Because people who have experienced trauma are absolutely attuned to everything. The example I can give you is one day we were standing and talking to a couple of parents who had been interpreters during the war for the Australian Defence Forces, and I shifted my foot and one of them jumped back, ready to take me down. They were so attuned to the way I was standing that when my foot turned, it looked like it could be taken more like, aggressively, more like a kind of a self-defence, that sort of thing. They jumped back. What does it say about the significance in really tiny things that occur that we don't think about, we don't regulate? And if you're going to work in these populations and get below a superficial trust, getting right down deep into it, that's the stuff that you have really got to look at and understand about yourself.*

> Context: I have been a principal in secondary school for the last 20 years. The school has Grades 7–12 with just over 1,000 enrolments, and we are in a small city. The school provides an extensive academic and vocational education curriculum to meet the needs of students. I maintain contact with those young people; I would say that 90% of them have very good jobs. Many of them are in trade, and in very good trades; some of them are nurses. Some of them are painters. Some of them are builders.

> *Some of my boys had been things like barbers in the refugee camps, and they would cut the teachers' hair, you know, you had this whole culture around these young people, and they were personalities. You had to build a culture with the other members of the staff, and the staff were the most resistant. The kids weren't, because*

*ultimately we had these boys stepping up and becoming school leaders in the school and sharing their experiences of what it was like. It enriched the whole school climate by having them there. It was just the most amazing experience for all the children who came in contact.*

### Unique contexts, global principles

Despite the great variance in the size of their schools, each of our principals shared understandings about the importance of truly being cognisant of the individual life experiences of every student and family they serve. The primary school principal from Australia has a wealth of experience in counselling and trauma and is keenly focused on understanding how his own behaviours affect others. His willingness to make every interaction a teachable moment for himself helped him to establish supportive and positive relationships across the school community. The secondary principal from Australia has a different set of challenges in attempting to support and educate young men for life beyond school. While keenly aware of their traumatic experiences, her positive narrative about the unique capacities and generosity and leadership traits of 'her boys' is indicative of a school culture that values the talents each of her students brings. Though leadership experience has certainly helped to ingrain their behaviours, our principals have made a conscious decision to engage with students and their families in every interaction in a very purposeful manner. The ability of these school leaders to genuinely empathise has translated into positive, connected school communities.

Empathy is as important for school leaders as it is often misunderstood. Creating a school culture of welcoming and belonging first demands a school principal who is capable of not simply feeling for others; it requires an individual to be deeply reflective about the potential and consequential effects of his or her behaviour. Principals must assess their conception of empathy in the first instance to determine if it is shaped by their own values and experiences. Principals should reflect on the role of power and privilege in their feeling of empathy. They need to explore if their knowledge of an individual's specific trauma leads them to feel more or less empathetic and if this knowledge potentially perpetuates a narrative of lower expectations and lower abilities. Finally, principals must work with their educators to address these very questions and explore opportunities to bring these understandings to their students. As our principals expressed, having clarity about one's understanding of empathy enables individuals to develop relationships that are honest and empowering. It is perhaps a fair observation that the way members of a school community regard children and families from refugee and asylum-seeker backgrounds is largely predicated on the principal's understanding and practice of empathy.

## Chapter conclusion

Developing a positive school culture, climate and ethos begins with understanding communities and their needs and then determining if school policies and practices support those needs. Conversations on the playground, home visits, potluck dinners and a host of other initiatives matter, but regular, purposeful collaboration with stakeholders to remain responsive to their needs is vital. This care for community needs to be the work of the entire school staff and principals can facilitate this by demonstrating care for their staff members. This includes hiring teachers who demonstrate an ethic of care, and frequently praising, recognising and rewarding staff members for their efforts to support students. Leaders must also practise and understand the concept of empathy. Understanding the importance of power, lived experiences and agency is key to practising empathy. Principals interviewed for this book use their understandings of empathy to shape each interaction with families in a purposeful, productive manner. It is evident that principals who continually reflect on their own thinking, who seek to be better, actually do better by the children and families they serve. In Chapter 6, the role of social safety, identity and integration are explored.

## References

Aldridge, J. M., Frazer, B., Fodzar, F., Ala'i, K., Earnest, J., & Afari, E. (2016). Students' perceptions of school climate as determinants of wellbeing, resilience and identity. *Improving Schools*, 19(1), 5–26. doi:10.1177/1365480215612616.

Bradshaw, C., Waarsdorp, T., Debnam, K., & Johnson, S. (2014). Measuring school climate in high schools: A focus on safety, engagement, and the environment. *Journal of School Health*, 84(9), 593–604.

Cohen, C., McCabe, E., Michelli, M., & Pickeral, T. (2009). School climate: Research, policy, practice and teacher education. *Teachers College Record*, 111(1), 183–213.

Cohen, J. (2006). Social, emotional, ethical, and academic education: Creating a climate for learning, participation in democracy, and well-being. *Harvard Educational Review*, 76(2), 201–237.

Cohen, T., Guffey, J., Higgins, S., & D'Alessandro, A. (2013). A review of school climate research. *Review of Educational Research*, 83(3), 357–385.

Davis, M. (1983). Measuring individual differences in empathy: Evidence for a multi-dimensional approach. *Journal of Personality and Social Psychology*, 44(1), 113–126.

Donnelly, C. (2000). In pursuit of school ethos. *British Journal of Educational Studies*, 48 (2), 134–154. www.jstor.org/stable/1556001?seq=1.

Erikson, F. (1987). Conceptions of school culture. *Education Administration Quarterly*, 23 (4), 11–24.

Ferfolja, T. (2009). The Refugee Action Support program: Developing understandings of diversity. *Teaching Education*, 20(4), 395–407. doi:10.1080/10476210902741239.

Ferfolja, T., & Vickers, M. (2010). Supporting refugee students in school education in Greater Western Sydney. *Critical Studies in Education*, 51(2), 149–162. doi:10.1080/ 17508481003731034.

Ferfolja, T., Diaz, C. J., & Ullman, J. (2018). *Understanding Sociological Theory for Educational Practices* (2nd ed.). Cambridge University Press.

Field, R., & Abelson, M. (1982). Climate: A reconceptualisation and proposed model. *Human Relations*, 35(3), 181–201.

Ford, D. Y. (2014). Why education must be multicultural: Addressing a few misperceptions with counterarguments. *Gifted Child Today*, 37(1), 59–62. doi:10.1177% 2F1076217513512304.

Freire, P. (1970). *Pedagogy of the Oppressed*. Continuum.

Glover, D., & Coleman, M. (2005). School culture, climate and ethos: Interchangeable or distinctive concepts? *Journal of In-Service Education*, 31(2), 251–272. www.tandfon line.com/doi/abs/10.1080/13674580500200278.

Gutstein, E., & Peterson, B. (2005). *Our history*. https://rethinkingschools.org/about-rethinking-schools/our-history/. https://rethinkingschools.org/about-rethinking-schools/our-history/.

Hopple, G., & Choi-Fitzpatrick, A. (2017). *Engineering Empathy: A Multidisciplinary Approach Combining Engineering, Peace Studies, and New Technology*. ASEE Annual Conference and Exposition, Columbus, Ohio.

Koss-Chioino, J. (2006). Spiritual transformation, relation and radical empathy: Core components of the ritual healing process. *Transcultural Psychiatry*, 43(4), 655–656.

Lampert, K. (2006). *Traditions of Compassion: From Religious Duty to Social Activism*. Palgrave Macmillan.

Loukas, A., & Robinson, S. (2004). Examining the moderating role of perceived school climate in early adolescent adjustment. *Journal of Research on Adolescence*, 14(2), 209–233.

Marsh, A. (2012). Empathy and compassion: A cognitive neuroscience perspective. In J. Decety (Ed.), *Empathy: From Bench to Bedside* (pp. 191–206). MIT Press.

Mirra, N. (2018). *Educating for Empathy*. Teachers College Press.

Noddings, N. (2012). *Philosophy of Education*. Westview Press.

Nussbaum, M. (2001). *Upheavals of Thought: The Intelligence of Emotions*. Cambridge University Press.

Ratcliffe, M. (2012). Phenomenology as a form of empathy. *Inquiry: An Interdisciplinary Journal of Philosophy*, 55(5), 474–495.

Solvason, C. (2005). Investigating specialist school ethos … Or do you mean culture? *Educational Studies*, 31(1), 85–94.

Walters, S. (2012). *School Climate: A Literature Review*. T. Associates.

# 6 Social safety, identity and integration

## Introduction

This chapter focuses on social safety for students with refugee and asylum-seeker backgrounds. Research on the concepts of identity, acculturation and integration is presented and the perspectives of school leaders from multiple countries are offered. In prior paradigms, individuals with refugee or asylum-seeker backgrounds or other marginalised populations were expected to 'assimilate' and shed their cultural backgrounds to become part of the new society they'd entered. Progressive school philosophies challenge that thinking through informed policies and practices that see these newly arrived students and families as assets to the community. This approach builds a rich new human experience for all students, staff and the broader school community.

## Acculturation

This term is frequently found in national and school policies, with little attention to subtle differences in its meaning, yet the expectations and implications of each are very different. Berry (1997, p. 7) discusses some of these differences, including the ambiguity of the original concept of acculturation, which referred to groups of individuals who had sustained close contact with groups from another culture without making it clear where the term was to be applied to changes in the newly arrived group culture (the acculturating group) or both this cohort and the group whose culture was acculturated to. He notes, however, that in practice, acculturating change is more extensive in one group than in the other in contexts where both are considered to have undergone changes as the result of their interactions with each other. He also gathers understandings from various sources which indicate that other, related vocabulary can also be defined in terms of their acculturating impacts. Based on historical notions of assimilation, this is defined as a particular type of acculturation that can be demonstrated in several ways. Describing these, he identifies (i) reactive, which instigates change in both cultural groups; (ii) creative, which is the catalyst for the development of a new cultural form, hitherto not found in either group; and (iii) delayed, which is change that can be acknowledged many years later.

DOI: 10.4324/9781003090731-6

Acculturation itself is a complex construct as it can be applied to groups of people who experience a change in the culture of the group, and to the individuals who comprise these groups as psychological acculturation. As with other groups in society, some individuals interact more successfully, more frequently and more positively than others in the same group. Consequently, the group may be found to have assimilated effectively, but that does not mean that all the individuals in that group have achieved the same degree of acculturation. Alitolppo-Niitama (2004, p. 84) highlights the importance of the individual nature of acculturation in her study of second-generation Somali-speaking communities in Helsinki. She indicates that there are many of the usual variables that impact on student success, including the human capital and any financial capital they can bring with them, the social capital that may relate to the capacities of themselves and their families to acculturate, the degree to which the new homeland society supports them in multiple contexts and their own human agency.

There exist some criticisms of Berry's studies of cross-cultural psychology; see for example Riedel et al. (2011) who resurrects the notion of salutogenesis, which stresses the capacities and resources of individuals to create health and wellbeing, and, in this case, considers this in relation to students with refugee and asylum-seeker experiences. Also, Rudmin (2003) critiques the four aspects of acculturation which comprise the foundational tenets of the model developed further by Berry (2001, p. 618), which are integration, separation, assimilation and marginalisation. Berry (2001) views the degree to which the heritage culture of these populations is maintained as resulting in acculturation, integration or separation. Groups who totally abandon their heritage culture are viewed as acculturated. Those who maintain their heritage cultures and avoid interaction with the receiving culture are considered to be separated and those who maintain their cultural heritage while interacting daily with their new cultural group are deemed to have been integrated. Those who have lost interest or have been forced to abandon their heritage culture and cannot interact with the majority culture, perhaps because of discrimination or racism, are believed to be marginalised.

A critical aspect of how these groups and individuals are able to acculturate is often determined by the degree of control that they have over the reasons for their migration. Refugees and asylum seekers have no choice and are rendered the most vulnerable in western societies, as are the students in schools (Berry, 1997; 2009; Berry, Horenczyk, et al., 2006; Berry, Phinney, et al., 2006; Doná & Berry, 1994; Ogbu, 1995a, 1995b). Berry (2001) suggests that the degree to which full integration can be achieved depends on the degree of authentic multiculturalism that exists in the receiving community and facilitates mutual accommodation. In contexts where the majority culture demands assimilation, the society becomes a 'melting pot' (Berry, 2001, pp. 619, 620). Where the majority culture demands separation, it becomes segregation. Groups who are unable to interact with either cultures for diverse reasons become marginalised and are therefore excluded from the receiving, major culture. In this way, acculturation is dependent on two variables: the heritage culture and majority culture of the receiving country. These basic understandings of acculturation and impacts of majority cultures are critical for understanding the culture of individual schools, the development of policies and the impacts of school leaders.

## Research findings

Our participants were extremely concerned about helping their newly arrived students join their new culture while also supporting their connection to their heritage culture. Two leaders, a primary principal in England and a primary principal in Australia, shared particularly poignant observations.

> Context: We have around 700 students; we have 90 per year group all the way from Reception up into Year 6. We're quite a big school. We serve a diverse community, and we do a lot of work with them; they're very supportive. In terms of student population, the community changes all the time. We used to have a lot of Eastern Europeans, but that seems to have changed over the years. I think I spoke to you about a refugee that we had, a Syrian lad; so, we have a lot of the Middle Eastern countries, Arabic countries, more of that now.

> *We've got very good procedures; we have a buddy system. First, we have senior leaders that meet and have an interview with the prospective new parents. We don't rely on our administration staff to do that, because we want our senior leaders to be asking the right questions, so we're getting the right answers. We want to have as much information as we possibly can. If the interview happens this week, the child will not start until the following week because we need to prepare resources, we need to ensure teachers are aware of that child, we need to chase up previous schools if need be, also conduct safeguarding, contact social workers. And for some of our refugee children that come they need contact with the person that's been supporting them. That gives us a week to gather as much information as we can. When the child comes in, they're shown around the school and they meet their teacher. The teacher often will have a welcome sign for that child and has already spoken to the class about this new child, regardless of where they come from and the child is bud-died up.*

> Context: I have been the principal here for 18 months. Currently in our school we have roughly 200 students enrolled. Within those 200 students, approximately 70% of children are English as Second Language or Dialect. And we have 12 or 13 languages that are spoken within our school. We have a really diverse community. Those children are from families who are asylum seekers, refugees, parents that are here doing a PhD at the university nearby.

*When they arrive, we set them up with a school uniform, we give them a bag, we give them a lunch box. We are very aware of their culture and that sometimes they love to wear long sleeves. Students talk about when they were back in their home country and a lot of our learning comes from that. We offer education programs in our school to provide some sort of way for parents to interact with other moms and dads within our community. For example, every Friday last year we had a coffee club. We had two interpreters at the coffee club, they came along, and they encouraged community mums and dads to come along. At those coffee clubs they discuss different topics: they looked at how to buy furniture, how to make a healthy meal on a budget, where do you have to go if you have to see a doctor. Because they don't have access to those things.*

### Unique contexts, global principles

Creating school environments where students with refugee and asylum-seeker backgrounds feel safe and accepted for who they are is a challenge for any school community. Our English primary principal has developed a rigorous and time-intensive approach for welcoming students that is founded on gathering as much information as possible prior to their enrolment. This principal involves multiple staff members in this process, facilitating schoolwide understanding and distributing the considerable effort involved. Of note, this principal also makes it a point to include prior teachers and social workers in this information gathering. By the time the student reaches his or her classroom, a welcome sign in their heritage language and a well-prepared teacher is waiting. As many of our participants advised, our Australian principal ensures the physical needs of her children with refugee and asylum-seeker backgrounds are met upon their entry to school. This even included modifying the school uniform to offer school-branded long-sleeve shirts and hijabs. This principal has created and resourced spaces and events in her school to allow families to gather and talk about their home countries and how to adapt to their new land. Her purposeful approach of funding two interpreters in a weekly coffee club for families demonstrates the school's commitment to supporting heritage cultures. Each of our principals demonstrate that a commitment to honouring heritage cultures while developing understanding of host cultures needs to be purposeful, well-resourced and embraced schoolwide.

Unlike a child arriving from another school, supporting children with refugee and asylum-seeker backgrounds is far more complex, far more work and much more of an emotional and professional load on school staff. Understanding where children come from, understanding their culture, their journeys and the amount of trauma they have experienced, contributes to helping the school prepare to support their wellbeing. As both of our principals demonstrate, leaders must not do this alone; rather, they need to incorporate their staff, prior teachers and external support workers in supporting these students. It is also vital to recognise the acculturation process will never be smooth as these students are attempting to live in two worlds and they are code-swapping and cultural swapping to survive. Our Australian example also illustrates the need to extend support to entire families. In doing so, schools are making a huge effort to respect and dignify cultures, to be inclusive, and setting up ways in which culture swapping can be enabled. By bringing community together and bringing community into schools, principals can do things to support parents to support their children.

## Identity

Earlier discussion indicated that the degree of social safety that students with refugee and asylum-seeker experiences can expect in schools is highly dependent on the culture of the school, the policies and their implementation and the degree of acceptance of multiculturalism that are embedded in these (Berry, 2001). Separation (segregation) or marginalisation are generally observed to be negative outcomes of acculturation into school communities as they inhibit or prohibit the sense of belonging, which is an important construct for the well-being of these students (Bradshaw et al., 2014; Loukas et al., 2006; Walters, 2012). However, in order to integrate, the groups of refugee and asylum-seeker populations need to have the energy and inclination to keep their heritage cultures alive in their new homelands. This is something that schools who embrace multiculturalism can encourage and support, both across the curriculum and in their community interactions. Berry et al. (2006) conducted a large-scale international study across 13 countries into the acculturation of immigrant youth. They sought to establish the ways in which the participating youth had acculturated to life in a new country and culture, using the four ways in which acculturation can be achieved: assimilation, separation, integration and marginalisation. The second goal was to investigate if there was any correlation between the ways in which the young people had acculturated and their psychological and sociocultural adaptation. The third goal of the study was to establish if there was any connection between the ways of acculturation and the levels of psychological and sociocultural adaptation. They also discriminated within groups, identifying participants by the length of residence in their new homeland.

They found that, despite the diversity in heritage culture and the new homeland culture and context, some strong trends emerged. They found the most common profile was the integration profile. These young people spoke their heritage language and the language of the majority culture, belonged to peer groups of both cultures and appeared to be comfortable with their identity, values and relationships in both heritage and national contexts, using both languages frequently. The second largest group were those with ethnic identity profiles, which indicated that these adolescents had acculturated by separating themselves from the majority culture, instead maintaining strong ties to their heritage cultures. The group who identified most strongly with the national culture was relatively small, indicating that fewer than expected had acculturated by assimilation. One atypical profile was identified. Nearly 1,000 young people reported high proficiency in heritage language but very low scores in heritage identity. They combined characteristics of assimilation, separation and marginalisation. Berry et al. named these participants as the 'diffuse' group as they reflected the characteristics of this group in the literature on identity formation who were 'characterised by a lack of commitment to a direction or purpose in their lives and often socially isolated (Marcia, 1994)' (in Berry et al., 2006, p. 316), although the residency data indicated that the longer-term residents had more positive outlooks.

The findings related to how well these young people had adapted indicated some powerful results that have implications for those who are in positions from which they can support successful adaptation. Berry et al. concluded that being involved with both cultures (integration strategy) resulted in better psychological and sociocultural adaptation. Conversely, lack of involvement in either culture, or being confused about ethnicity as in the diffuse group, was found to be unsupportive of both psychological and sociocultural adaptation, as would be anticipated by marginalised acculturation. Separation proved to be relatively supportive of adaptation in both areas, while an orientation towards the national profile was less supportive of both psychological and sociocultural adaptation. The most positive outcomes for immigrant youth were integration and separation as they both provided strong identity profiles, the most supportive overall being the integration pathway to acculturation. Assimilation was less supportive of both types of adaptation and marginalisation was unsupportive of both. The implications are clear for principals and school leaders. While many well-meaning educators may advocate for assimilation strategies to support their newcomer students, it is those who embrace the cultural diversity and celebrate the many differences in knowing and doing who are providing the most positive adaptation contexts and interactions for these young people. Additionally, these school leaders are respecting the distinct ontologies and epistemologies of the heritage cultures of students with refugee and asylum-seeker experiences as integral to their identity formation while simultaneously engaging them with the majority or national culture.

### Research findings

Our participants were keenly focused on understanding and respecting the heritage cultures of their students. Two educators who spoke extensively about this were a primary principal in Northern Ireland and a leader in New Zealand.

> Context: I was a member of the senior management team and special needs coordinator for my school (Nursery-P7). I am now doing my PhD studentship full time but I'm also doing some associate lecturing at a teacher education college. This means I teach modules with fourth-year students, in which I focus on supporting newcomer people. Newcomer people: that's what they're termed in Northern Ireland; I absolutely hate the word.

*Again, this is my personal opinion. I think probably what teachers needed most, to be honest with you, wasn't the resources. It was a little bit of empathy and a bit of intercultural understanding and awareness. In Northern Ireland we're probably not the most welcoming of people. Here is an area where our students, where people in general, are quite guarded and there is a lot of suspicion of others. I think maybe at the beginning when numbers were quite small people were more open, more welcoming and warmer. Certainly, in the local area over the years where there are higher numbers of refugees and asylum seekers, you do get that little bit of narrative, maybe not among the teachers but certainly among some of the support staff. Some of the canteen ladies and cleaners say things such as, "our housing is being taken." That is the kind of narrative, and people talk, or you will hear things like, "they get everything given to them for free," that kind of thing.*

Context: I'm a primary trained teacher. I have a Teachers of English to Speakers of Other Languages qualification and a Master's in Applied Language Studies. Now, I'm involved in managing an organisation that funds more than 50,000 students a year who are English-language learners. So, I manage the people and the funding; we distribute some of that funding specifically for refugees and some of it for all English-language learners.

*I say to people, "please encourage and support students' first languages because that's absolutely vital to the sense of wellbeing, identity and belonging." It's not obvious to some people, but all the research evidence shows us that students who are strong in their first language will excel in English. Now, that's quite tricky for refugees because I understand that many of them will not be literate in the first language. But they will probably be able to... orally, they'll be fine speaking and listening. It's about knowing that. I say to people, "Do you know what languages they speak? Do you know what they can read, what they can understand, what they can write? Do you know that and are you building on that?" It is all about really knowing your learners and adapting your teaching programs to include the learners' knowledge, languages and cultures. I really encourage and support the learning of a first language.*

### Unique contexts, global principles

Integration and acceptance of children and families with refugee and asylum-seeker backgrounds is a challenge for any school community. Our primary principal from Northern Ireland is an example of an individual working in a particularly difficult host environment marred by historical violence and discrimination. His observation that empathy and intercultural understanding of newly arrived families was more needed by his staff than material resources is illustrative of his challenge. While he has made positive gains with his teachers, he faces much greater resistance from his support staff members, individuals likely more inclined to see newly arrived families as threats to their own economic wellbeing. Our leader from New Zealand is direct about the need to

respect and encourage students to use their heritage language. Doing so supports student wellbeing and furthers their sense of belonging. Just as important,
this leader challenges her staff members to not only encourage students to speak
in their heritage language but also to find out as much as they can about their
students' languages, cultures and prior knowledge. While each of these leaders
put great effort on helping their newly arrived students find a place in their
school community, they also emphasised educating their community to better
understand their newly arrived residents.

These vignettes illustrate a challenging reality for school leaders. While some
regions or entire nations may be more inclined to welcome families with
refugee and asylum-seeker backgrounds, others may be predisposed to be
unwelcoming based on difficult regional histories or economic realities. The
principal in Northern Ireland is working to help his newly arrived students
both maintain their identity and find their place in his school in the face of an
unwelcoming community that experienced decades of civil unrest. This vignette underscores findings in Chapter 4 that indicate suffering historical trauma
does not make an individual more inclined to be accepting or appreciative of
others. The New Zealand example also contains a host of fundamental lessons
about helping newly arrived families maintain their identity while integrating
into society. In many schools, for supposedly developmental reasons, educators
have limited or eliminated the ability of students to communicate in their
heritage language. Language is vital to student wellbeing. Language is part of
who they are, and we damage their capacity for development when we prohibit them from using their heritage language. Schools must encourage learning
through both heritage and host language, and they must encourage families to
maintain use of the heritage language while also learning the host language.
The important learnings from our two leaders emanate from their purposeful
effort to understand and respect every member of their school community.

## Integration

As the work from Berry (2001, 2009; Berry et al., 2006) and his associates has
illustrated, the perspective on assimilation of refugee and asylum seekers has
changed considerably since the 1960s. Principals and their communities are
now challenged to integrate these cohorts of students into their mainstream
schools and existing cultures while encouraging parents and students to engage
with their heritage languages and cultural customs and beliefs. It is no longer
sufficient to think or act as though heritage can be accommodated outside of
school contexts if students are to be integrated into these educational communities. Authentic school integration can contribute considerably to the psychological and sociocultural adaptation and wellbeing of these student populations.
In order to achieve this, school principals and entire communities need to view
students as assets, to value the contributions they can make to intercultural and
multicultural understandings and appreciation of difference and to the inherent
value of diverse ontologies and epistemologies. While some schools include

annual cultural days and occasional incursions and excursions, it is the principals who ensure that the cultural diversity in the school is celebrated in the classroom contexts of teaching and learning, on the playgrounds (Kugler & Price, 2009) and in all school interactions with parents and communities (Madziva & Thondhlana, 2017), who are making a difference and demonstrating a deep understanding of integration. They manage this despite the constraints under which they work (Hanna, 2013), which can impact negatively on students' parity of participation in schools (Keddie, 2012). In contexts of extreme homogeneity, this may need careful structuring, preparation and consistent modelling by the principal and his staff, but integration means that these students must be visible and contribute to the culture of the school, in addition to impacting upon it. Integration also means that more attention needs to be paid to the ways in which these students are able to participate and express their learning, acknowledging that learner identities are critical aspects of successful adaptation (Bal, 2014).

Many ethical, sociological, psychological and creative pedagogical (Rahmawati, 2012; Rousseau et al., 2005; Vickers & McCarthy, 2010) interventions have been operationalised to support the successful learning identities of these students. Alford (2014) discusses the importance of interrupting the deficit discourse (Uptin et al., 2016) that dominates in some schools about the skills and experiences of students with refugee and asylum-seeker backgrounds. Investigating classroom practices that facilitated the inclusion of knowledge and understandings as the focal point of lessons, she highlights the particular difficulties of these learners as they struggle to learn complex intellectual material in the senior years and express it in a language they have barely mastered. Arizpe et al. (2014) adopt a framework of visual literacy based on Freire's notion of 'generative themes' in illustrated literature, placing these students at the centre of the classroom knowledge and discussions, and supporting the development of intercultural understandings. Emert (2014) and Vecchio et al. (2017) also reported the use of visuals and digital storytelling as being successful, focusing on students' previous experiences as starting points for learning (Miller et al., 2014). Block et al. (2014, p. 1348) reported similar findings, quoting a principal who appreciated the influence these cohorts had on the school as a whole. She states:

> A number of interview participants reported benefits for non-refugee-background students as well as refugee-background students from participation in the programme. As one school leader expanded:
> … like being more tolerant and culturally diverse in the things that we celebrate in the school; trying to be more inclusive in the curriculum; trying to identify students who may have some background that may involve us needing to make sure [the student] wellbeing [team in the school] is at least aware [of them] … (Leadership, Secondary School)

While providing integrative experiences may be challenging for principals, the integrative process also provides a challenge for students with refugee and asylum-seeker experiences. Balancing between two worlds, two languages, two cultures has been shown to support increased psychological and sociocultural adaptation; these students need all the support they can get at school (Das, 2019; Gibson, 2010).

### Research findings

Our participants were concerned about the role of the school in helping to integrate children and families with refugee and asylum-seeker experiences. Two leaders who shared insightful observations were a primary principal in Northern Ireland and a primary principal in New Zealand.

> Context: We have about 18 countries represented here at the school (Nursery-P7). I've been teaching for 21 years. I'm coming to the end of my fifth year as principal and I was vice principal in a smaller school for seven years before that. Our school has around 270 students and of those students, about 30% are newcomers.

> *When this student talks about Arabic, she says, "Oh, that's the language my mummy speaks." All her conversation is using English; she's so expressive, and she's so happy. When you see her in school, you kind of think to yourself, "this child has been here all her life" or at least you would believe that. The change from day one until now is absolutely enormous. She speaks Arabic very well, but to her, her first language is English. We never discourage a child; I mean, we never encourage a child to move towards English as being their main language. Yes, we want them to speak English, but we would really like them to be able to speak their own language and be very bright in their own language.*

> Context: We have around 750 Students (Grades 1–6) with 70 ethnicities. We are one of the most diverse schools in New Zealand. I've been a principal now for 13 years, and in education for 23–24 years, at a range of schools both independent and public. This is my third stint as a principal. Honestly, it's fantastic to work in such a diverse place every day.

> *Probably the major impact or the major change that we've really made over the last three years has been to really embrace the children's first languages, cultures and families. I'm really making more than a token effort to understand them as learners and as people. But then, there's a lot of things we didn't understand at first. The parents didn't come along because often there would be other males in meetings or there would be other people that they didn't feel comfortable sharing with, or their husbands at that stage wouldn't allow them to go. We've had a number of barriers that we weren't even aware were barriers. Now we break that initial ice; people then feel comfortable coming to the school, having learned in conversations who to speak to, if they need to. In another example, we discovered that many of our Somali girls were not taking up swimming at school and making all sorts of excuses and things.*

*With support from our English-language learner coordinator, the mums would come along and watch how the daughters were being treated. We did two separate sessions, with sons and daughters separated. So, there have been lots of different layers to our success; we now incorporate a lot of the diversity of our student population right through to the strategic planning, which has deliberate actions we take to engage with the community.*

### Unique contexts, global principles

Each of our principals made it a point to really try to understand their students and to encourage them to be themselves. Our principal from Northern Ireland was clearly proud of the academic, social and emotional growth his young student exhibited. While the little girl was pleased with her English facility and associated Arabic with her mother, the principal was quick to draw attention to the fact his team would never discourage a child to use their heritage language. In fact, this principal made it clear he would like to see his students with refugee and asylum-seeker backgrounds maintain and excel in this heritage language. Our primary principal from New Zealand has, in recent years, come to realise the importance of embracing heritage languages, cultures and families. His purposeful efforts to get to know newly arrived families were met with challenges and new understandings. Making an effort to be more aware led this principal to uncover many problems to which he was previously blind. This principal's realisation his Somali girls were not joining swimming class due to gender issues prompted him to make changes and restructure the class, a step he would likely not have taken for his native students. Creating places where students feel welcome and safe, as our two examples illustrate, requires responsive principals who encourage students to be themselves.

It is important to remember children with refugee and asylum-seeker backgrounds did not choose to leave their homeland and encouraging them to remain engaged in their heritage culture is a healthy way to help them integrate on their own terms. While schools clearly need to focus on English language acquisition for newly arrived students, the understanding that heritage languages are just as valuable for integration must be shared by all staff members. Principals and their teachers can support this integration by learning as much as possible about heritage cultures and being as accommodating as feasible. In some cases, as our New Zealand swimming example illustrates, this accommodation means schools changing policies and practices to address cultural mores. Principals should strive to create environments where heritage and host cultures permeate all aspects of schooling and where heritage cultures are known and valued.

## Chapter conclusion

Creating environments where children and families with refugee and asylum-seeker backgrounds are welcomed and valued is a challenge for any school community. In many cases, as a result of historical events or cultural issues, the context in which school leaders are working can exacerbate this challenge. As a step towards ameliorating this, principals interviewed for this book emphasised the need to help their communities view newly arrived individuals as assets rather than challenges. In addition to bringing unique cultures and languages, students with refugee experience bring resilience, determination and grit, having survived years of conflicts, refugee camps, trauma and loss. Reflective principals take the time to come to know these students and families deeply and they respect and encourage these individuals to maintain their culture and their language. These principals recognise that assimilation and acculturation are two-way processes and school communities change and grow for the better as a result of the diversity of students they serve. The attributes of effective leadership for shaping welcoming schools are discussed in Chapter 7.

## References

Alford, J. H. (2014). "Well, hang on, they're actually much better than that!": Disrupting dominant discourses of deficit about English language learners in senior high school English. *English Teaching: Practice & Critique (University of Waikato)*, 13(3), 71–88. https://files.eric.ed.gov/fulltext/EJ1050176.pdf.

Alitolppo-Niitama, A. (2004). Somali youth in the context of schooling in metropolitan Helsinki: A framework for assessing variability in educational performance. *Journal of Ethnic and Migration Studies*, 30(1), 81–106.

Arizpe, E., Bagelman, C., Devlin, A. M., Farrell, M., & McAdam, J. E. (2014). Visualizing intercultural literacy: Engaging critically with diversity and migration in the classroom through an image-based approach. *Language and Intercultural Communication*, 14(3), 304–321. doi:10.1080/14708477.2014.903056.

Bal, A. (2014). Becoming in/competent learners in the United States: Refugee students' academic identities in the figured world of difference. *International Multilingual Research Journal*, 8(4), 271–290. doi:10.1080/19313152.2014.952056.

Berry, J. (1997). Immigration, acculturation, and adaptation. *Applied Psychology: An International Review*, 46(1), 5–68.

Berry, J. (2001). A psychology of immigration. *Journal of Social Issues*, 7(3), 615–631.

Berry, J. (2009). A critique of critical acculturation. *International Journal of Intercultural Relations*, 33(5), 361–371. doi:10.1016/j.ijintrel.2009.06.003.

Berry, J. W., Horenczyk, G., & Kwak, K. (2006). *Immigrant Youth in Cultural Transition: Acculturation, Identity, and Adaptation across National Contexts*. Lawrence Erlbaum Associates.

Berry, J., Phinney, J., Sam, D., & Vedder, P. (2006). Immigrant youth: Acculturation, identity, and adaptation. *Applied Psychology: An International Review*, 55(3), 303–332.

Block, K., Cross, S., Riggs, E., & Gibbs, L. (2014). Supporting schools to create an inclusive environment for refugee students. *International Journal of Inclusive Education*, 18(12), 1337–1355. doi:10.1080/13603116.2014.899636.

Bradshaw, C., Waarsdorp, T., Debnam, K., & Johnson, S. (2014). Measuring school climate in high schools: A focus on safety, engagement, and the environment. *Journal of School Health*, 84(9), 593–604.

Das, M. (2019). Between two worlds: An immigrant story. *Humanity & Society*, 43(3), 327–345. doi:10.1177/0160597618784732.

Doná, G., & Berry, J. W. (1994). Acculturation attitudes and acculturative stress of Central American refugees. *International Journal of Psychology*, 29(1), 57–70.

Emert, T. (2014). "Hear a story, tell a story, teach a story": Digital narratives and refugee middle schoolers. *Voices from the Middle*, 21(4), 33–39. https://library.ncte.org/journals/vm/issues/v21-4/25107.

Gibson, J. (2010, February 13). Trapped between two worlds. *Sydney Morning Herald*. www.smh.com.au/national/trapped-between-two-worlds-20100212-nxm8.html.

Hanna, P. L. (2013). Conflicts of interest: A case study exploring constraints on educational leaders' agency as representatives of refugee interests. *Leadership and Policy in Schools*, 12(2), 146–173. doi:10.1080/15700763.2013.815783.

Keddie, A. (2012). Refugee education and justice issues of representation, redistribution and recognition. *Cambridge Journal of Education*, 42(2), 197–212. doi:10.1080/0305764x.2012.676624.

Kugler, E., & Price, O. (2009). *Helping immigrant and refugee students succeed: It's not just what happens in the classroom.* www.ilctr.org/wp-content/uploads/2017/12/Helping-immigrant-and-refugee-students-succeed.pdf.

Loukas, A., Suzuki, R., & Horton, K. (2006). Examining school connectedness as a mediator of school climate effects. *Journal of Research on Adolescence*, 16(3), 491–502 doi:10.1111/j.1532-7795.2006.00504.x.

Madziva, R., & Thondhlana, J. (2017). Provision of quality education in the context of Syrian refugee children in the UK: Opportunities and challenges. *Compare: A Journal of Comparative and International Education*, 47(6), 942–961. doi:10.1080/03057925.2017.1375848.

Miller, J., Windle, J. A., & Yazdanpanah, L. K. (2014). Planning lessons for refugee-background students: Challenges and strategies. *International Journal of Pedagogies & Learning*, 9(1), 38–48. doi:10.5172/ijpl.2014.9.1.38.

Ogbu, J. (1995a). Cultural problems in minority education: Their interpretations and consequences—Part one: Theoretical background. *The Urban Review*, 27, 189–205.

Ogbu, J. (1995b). Cultural problems in minority education: Their interpretations and consequence—Part two: The case studies. *The Urban Review*, 27, 271–297.

Rahmawati, Y. (2012). *Revealing and Reconceptualising Teaching Identity through the Landscapes of Culture, Religion, Transformative Learning, and Sustainability Education: A Transformation Journey of a Science Educator.* Curtin University of Technology, Australia.

Riedel, J., Weismann, U., & Hannich, H.-J. (2011). An integrative theoretical framework of acculturation and salutogenesis. *International Review of Psychiatry*, 23(6), 555–564. doi:10.3109/09540261.2011.637912.

Rousseau, C., Drapeau, A., Lacroix, L., Bagilishya, D., & Heusch, N. (2005). Evaluation of a classroom program of creative expression workshops for refugee and immigrant children. *Journal of Child Psychology and Psychiatry*, 46(2), 180–185. doi:10.1111/j.1469-7610.2004.00344.x.

Rudmin, F. (2003). Critical history of the acculturation psychology of assimilation, separation, integration, and marginalization. *Review of General Psychology*, 7(1), 3–37.

Uptin, J., Wright, J., & Harwood, V. (2016). Finding education: Stories of how young former refugees constituted strategic identities in order to access school. *Race Ethnicity and Education*, 19(3), 598–617. doi:10.1080/13613324.2014.885428.

Vecchio, L., Dhillon, K. K., & Ulmer, J. B. (2017). Visual methodologies for research with refugee youth. *Intercultural Education*, 28(2), 131–142. doi:10.1080/14675986.2017.1294852.

Vickers, M. H., & McCarthy, F. E. (2010). Repositioning refugee students from the margins to the centre of teachers' work. *International Journal of Diversity in Organisations, Communities & Nations*, 10(2), 199–210. https://doi.org/10.18848/1447-9532/CGP/v10i02/39838.

Walters, S. (2012). *School climate: A literature review*. Temescal Associates. https://docplayer.net/21010292-School-climate-a-literature-review.html.

# 7 Leadership and school culture

## Introduction

The body of research on the attitudes, behaviours and dispositions of effective school leaders is rich. Recommendations from virtually every study encourage leaders to build a culture of trust, transparency, engagement and empowerment. Surprisingly, these recommendations make it seem relatively easy to build such a school culture. This chapter highlights the challenges and benefits of developing a positive culture and shares strategies from principals working in multiple countries. These school leaders recognise that for children and families with refugee and asylum-seeker backgrounds, feeling welcome, supported and safe in their host school community is foundational for their personal and academic success.

## The importance of positive thinking

As the work of school principals becomes increasingly complex, multi-faceted and challenging, the importance of positive thinking becomes more important for a number of reasons. Positivity can help build welcoming school climates, develop cultures of confidence in the face of difficulties and permeate the ethos of the school. That is not to suggest that there will be no adversity to overcome, no arduous encounters or problematic issues to face, but research, especially that which investigates the working of the brain, can now indicate just how important and powerful deliberate, positive thinking can be. A whole-school approach to positivity can help alleviate the effect of trauma and loss for refugee and asylum-seeker students, encourage parents and communities to become involved in school interactions and sustain the work of the staff who support students in their own individual ways everyday inside and outside of classrooms. Fredrickson (2000, 2001) investigated the impact of positive emotion on the brain with the aid of *fMRI* scanning. This type of imaging, in contrast to *MRI* scanning, shows the metabolic functioning in the various sections of the brain. In this way, areas of increased brain activity can not only be observed but can be captured in the areas of the brain that are stimulated by various emotions. She found that after experiencing positive emotions of hope,

DOI: 10.4324/9781003090731-7

joy, pride, happiness, contentment and love, her research participants had increased activity across areas on both sides of the brain. She commented that in follow-up activities, these emotions had the capacity to 'broaden people's momentary thought – action repertoires, widening the array of the thoughts and actions that come to mind' (2001, p. 3) and that the participants were creative and open to varying perspectives and strategies for task completion. She also found that after experiencing emotions of fear, distress, hatred and other negative feelings, not only were the brain's regions less active and in fewer areas, but the participants were less inclined to be adventurous or creative in follow-up activities, preferring to consider only one perspective and not multiple. This, and other studies, indicate the neurological impact of fear as discussed in Chapter 4, and the potential of positive experiences in teaching and learning contexts.

Fredrickson's work builds on the work of others in the field, including that of Csikszentmihalyi (1988, 1991a, 1991b; Csikszentmihalyi & Lebuda, 2017) and the notion of the optimal human experience, which he describes as 'flow'. Pushing back against reductionist theories which sought to explain human behaviours scientifically, instead of recognising multiple factors that can explain or motivate individual actions (Dupré & O'Neill, 1998), Csikszentmihalyi focused on the development of an individual's sense of 'self'. He argued that, once the notion of 'self' is established in the conscious mind, then it seeks its own survival. Many of these notions of self are genetically or culturally determined. However, Csikszentmihalyi's work explored the extreme positive response, 'a condition of consciousness known as negentropy, optimal experience or flow… is obtained when all the components of consciousness are in harmony with each other, and with the goals that define a person's self' (1988, p. 24.). He posits that power, participation and pleasure are not sufficient motivators for the goals that are undertaken by some individuals, and that instead, they are motivated by exhilarating, positive experiences that are sought out time and time again. Indicating that these goals then become part of a sense of self, he names this 'autotelic motivation' (1988, p. 28): the task is done for its own sake, not for any reward or product as the experience is in the process, not in the task itself. Interestingly, irrespective of many areas of diversity, the impact of the task being undertaken is similar. Individuals become oblivious to the many distractions in their environment and engage in the task with totally focused consciousness, disregarding the passage of time, problems that arise and any self-consciousness. Additionally, in order to repeat the 'flow' experience, tasks must have the same degree of harmony with other components of consciousness but need to become more difficult at each step. In order to engage in 'flow', individuals need to have strong, accurate self-knowledge. This is because tasks that are too easy result in boredom or apathy and tasks that are too difficult create feelings of frustration and anxiety.

One of the most important implications of the theory of 'flow' was evidenced by Csikszentmihalyi's (1988) research participants. These were disenfranchised, disillusioned teenagers who had dropped out of school without any

formal academic qualifications. As participation was voluntary, these participants retained sufficient curiosity (generated by positive emotion) to become
part of the study and to nominate tasks they felt suited their interests and skills.
As can be discovered later in the chapter, these participants, perhaps in
common with some of the refugee and asylum-seeker students in schools,
challenged the preconceptions of 'intelligence' as being the hallmark of success
at school and a prerequisite for success, demonstrating not only a capacity for
learning successfully given the opportunity, but also, critically, the capability to
engage positively if tasks are designed so that they can use their relative
strengths to be successful. It is positively and potentially autotelic motivation
that characterises the work of principals who successfully support the needs of
students with refugee and asylum-seeker experiences as these roles are more
intensive, more complicated and more involved: they depend heavily on tasks
to be undertaken that are in 'harmony with other components of the conscious
self and with the goals that define their personal selves' (Csikszentmihalyi,
1988, p. 24).

## Research findings

Our participants articulated a strong belief in the students with whom they are
working and a need to remain positive. Two leaders who were particularly
focused on unleashing their students' potential were a primary principal in New
Zealand and a high school principal in Australia.

> Context: A large primary school, from Year 1 to 8, which means we have
> students from 5 years old to 13 years old. We've got a large school for the
> area, probably about 520 children here. I've been the principal here for
> nearly 20 years. We are quite diverse, and when I say diverse culturally, we
> have 20 different cultures here but not large numbers of some cultures.
> We have roughly 20% Maori, about 5% Pasifika and then we have a lot of
> other cultures.

> *In New Zealand, we talk about a thing called Whakamna, that means to build a
> relationship on a street; it's basically to do with parents. When you see them, you
> immediately say something positive about the child. You know, we often only hear
> from teachers when there's something going or gone wrong. So, I encourage my staff
> that when you see parents you should be saying, "Hey, did you know, I read a
> really great piece of writing the other day or did you know your child could act like
> that?" or whatever it is you know about that child, whatever is actually going to be
> meaningful... It's a big school, but we want to know as many of the children and
> know them as really well we can. We know what works for them, what doesn't
> work for them, what will make things move forward for them.*

> Context: My school is a high school (Years 7–12) with roughly 550
> enrolments. Our enrolments kind of follow the hotspots of the world, in

terms of where the war zones are. We're a very multicultural place. I think
we have 90% students who are non-English-speaking background. We
have about 60 different cultural groups across the schools. That's pretty
massive. Arabic is the major language group, but we have multiple cultures
within that language group.

*I'm a maths teacher and some of the refugee boys who love Mathematics like I do;*
*I've connected with them really well. To see them get into university and study*
*science and engineering and things like that is just phenomenal. So, there's a whole*
*range of those success stories. Then there's the other kind of success stories I love.*
*When, not just with refugee kids but there's a couple in this category, they actually*
*leave in Year 10 but they get an apprenticeship and they're brilliant at it. School*
*was wrong for them. They're angry at school; they're frustrated at school. There are*
*all these ridiculous rules. They've just been fending for themselves for years in*
*ghettos, and now I want to tell them to wear a school jumper. They must think,*
*"Get off it, that's ridiculous," but when you when you break through that and*
*work with them, and then transition them into an apprenticeship or something that's*
*a fantastic success. Although part of them would recognise, I didn't even finish Year*
*10, but who cares? The kid's happy, the family's happy. I'm terrible with names,*
*but I can see the faces of the boys that have done those sorts of journeys, and they*
*are the success stories I love.*

### Unique contexts, global principles

Each of our leaders shared insights about the power of positive interactions
with children and families with refugee and asylum-seeker backgrounds. Our
New Zealand primary principal is purposeful in each of her meetings with
parents to begin with a compliment about their child. She sets a positive tone
for every parental interaction, demonstrates a wealth of knowledge about her
students and has also established the importance of an asset-based approach to
her staff. This principal is focused on her staff knowing as much as possible
about each of the school's students as she contends this helps every student to
progress. Our Australian leader offers an example of a principal supporting
students beyond academics and the traditional expectations of schooling. She
works hard to know her students and find the unique talents of each and she
maintains a healthy outlook about what she deems 'ridiculous' school policies
and expectations. This principal is always cognisant of the trauma and inhu-
mane experiences her newly arrived students have experienced and this gives
her perspective. In fact, when appropriate, she celebrates her students leaving
school early, finding trades and leading successful lives. Both principals are
consistently positive about their students and it is also evident they each work
hard to know their students beyond a superficial understanding.

Creating positive relationships and positive environments is vital for students
who are experiencing negativity, feelings of distress and hopelessness. Principals
must work with the whole-school culture to know about every child and to

promote their wellbeing and success. This is a tremendous effort to undertake but one that creates a culture of acceptance, support and genuine interest in each child. To extend this practice, as our New Zealand principal did, to communicate positives to parents challenges the way schools typically operate and the ways families typically view schools. Our Australian high school principal offers keen insight into the importance of leaders helping students thrive inside and outside of school. For students who may have lost much of their childhood fending for their families or themselves in refugee camps, many of the conventions of schooling may prove too foreign or inane. Helping these students find their path outside of K-12 education is every bit a success for proactive school leaders. Principals who demonstrate to their students and their staff members a willingness to challenge school norms for the benefit of their students create a culture of positivity.

## Principals' perceptions of the nature of intelligence

Remaining positive when attempting to support students who have refugee and asylum-seeker experiences may prove to be particularly challenging for principals and teachers. Displacement itself is considered to be a traumatic event, causing as it does a loss of a sense of belonging for these students and their communities. Displacement 'dismantles the emotional, spiritual and physical connections with place' (Frater-Mathieson, 2004, p. 12) and may contribute to health problems in general, in addition to being an underestimated factor in the negative experiences discussed in Chapter 4 as trauma and loss for these students and their communities. School policies and interactions need to remain both positive and informed, as trauma-related classroom behaviours of these groups of students may be problematic for teachers (Blackwell & Melzak, 2000), especially if they are focused on what generally constitutes 'good' behaviour in western classrooms (MacLure et al., 2012). Mthethwa-Sommers and Kisiara (2015), Rutter and Jones (1998) and McMichael et al. (2011) are among a number of theorists who investigate the wider impact of refugee and asylum-seeker experiences and their subsequent impact on student behaviours, recommending strategies for positive actions in addition to the pedagogical approaches and considerations discussed in Chapter 8. One of the most basic professional influences on teacher responses and understandings of students and their potential is their perception of the nature of intelligence (Sellars, 2017). This is particularly pertinent in relation to students with refugee and asylum-seeker experiences as they are frequently perceived as 'deficit' (see, for example, Alford, 2014; Uptin et al., 2016), a view frequently resulting from previous schooling experiences, lack of English skills and other personal and cultural characteristics.

There exist many theories of intelligence, including those that propose intelligence as a fixed, general intelligence (Horn & Cattell, 1967; Spearman, 1904), which, although widely criticised for their lack of acknowledgement of the influence of social and cultural influences, are still the criteria used for identifying the need for specialist support funding by many education systems. Other views of the nature of intelligence include those who position it as broad competencies across many areas (for example, Thurstone, 1938), those who acknowledge social and cultural values in determining what it is to be intelligent in a multi-faceted model (for example, Gardner, 1983) and those who identify different types of intelligence commonly exhibited in educational contexts (see, for example, Sternberg & Kaufman, 1998). However, one of the interpretations of intelligence that has had a considerable impact on student performance is that elaborated by Dweck (2006), who posited that the beliefs individuals held about the nature of intelligence were directly related to their success or failure. She proposes that individuals who believe that intelligence is a fixed entity, genetically determined and unchangeable, are challenged by inevitable failure, lack persistence, make excuses for their lack of success and are readily defeated. She strongly advocates the possibilities and potential of a more positive approach, which she labels a 'growth mindset'. Conversely, individuals who embrace intelligence as a construct that is not predetermined but is capable of becoming stronger and facilitating increased success with hard work and motivation are more likely to be more persistent, view challenges and failure as learning opportunities and engage more fully in the learning process with positivity and determination. While this perspective of intelligence may be reminiscent of Bandura (1986) and his work on self-efficacy, in this case specifically applied to the nature of intelligence, research has indicated that encouraging students to develop a 'growth mindset' about themselves as intelligent individuals has proven to facilitate greater success and to prompt students to be positively motivated and resilient in relation to challenging tasks. This may prove to be a critical mindset for students with refugee and asylum-seeker experiences as they enter school environments without the language, cultural understandings and school experiences of their new homelands. This aspect of positive thinking may be an ideal tool for school principals to articulate as schoolwide policy and for teachers to adopt in their classrooms as the diversity of students with refugee and asylum-seeker backgrounds increases and their accountability intensifies.

### Research findings

For students entering schools where the dominant language is foreign, where cultural expectations are new and where school conventions are alien, remaining positive about learning can be a challenge. Principals in our research offered a growth perspective on learning and two who stood out were a primary principal in the United States and a high school principal in New Zealand.

> Context: My school is pre-Kindergarten – Fifth Grade. I know I'm the most diverse elementary school in the county; we're probably one of the most diverse in the state. We have 1,000 students, with 100% qualifying for free or reduced lunch. We have over 100 newcomers every year at my

school and a large immigrant population as well. Our largest student population is Hispanic; after that it is students from the Middle East.

*I think for me, the biggest thing needed is an open mind. In terms of some of the skills that are needed to help English-language learners succeed, you can learn those and you can continue to learn those and grow, but if you have a mindset that these kids cannot learn, or it is not my fault and I do not need to help them, then there is nothing we can do to help you teach them. Because I noticed that with a lot of teachers. But if you come in with an open mindset, thinking, "there are things that I can learn, I can help these kids," then we can help you to develop strategies that will help them. Our test scores did not go up the first year. Parents were happy the first year, kids were happy, staff was happy the first year, but some of these other results did not happen the first year. That took a little bit longer, so you have to be committed for the long haul.*

Context: My school is Years 9 to 13 (ages 13 to 18), with roughly 1,400 students. I've been in my role now for about 16 years. I've had students come through and now their families are also coming through. There's quite an established Congolese community and quite an established Burmese or Myanmar community. In another role, I have also been responsible for developing training for principals and teachers of refugee students.

*We think sometimes refugee-background students can be almost considered a problem, rather than a group of people who have the potential to majorly enrich others' lives and also excel academically in their own lives. I guess it's the disposition as much as anything because you can learn content, but you can't learn kindness. We can, but sometimes people don't. There are many elements to be a welcoming school, in terms of addressing racism, understanding being inclusive, welcoming, encouraging etc. And then there are other things that go into being a welcoming classroom, actual practical resources and knowing the impact of a break in a student's education. I think ultimately the staff should reflect the communities. So, I think if somebody came from those communities as a teacher, it's huge…*

### Unique contexts, global principles

Both of our principals were purposeful in the way they spoke about individuals' capacity for learning and the importance of being positive. Our principal from the United States focuses on helping her staff members develop and maintain a growth mindset. This principal has developed a whole-school approach in which she makes clear that staff members who believe in the potential of English-language learners will have the support they need to effect change. She also offers a thoughtful perspective on learning and test scores indicating parent, staff and student happiness was a key metric in the first year after her school started accepting children with refugee and asylum-seeker backgrounds. Our high school principal from New Zealand is keenly aware of the importance of the school community and the deleterious effects that unkind staff members can have on newly arrived students. She is assertive about the need for staff to see a refugee background as enriching the school culture, as opposed to a problem or a limitation. This principal recognises that a schoolwide belief system is needed but it must be implemented at the classroom level with effective pedagogical practices, teacher understanding and necessary resources. She also shares a keen observation about the need to hire staff members who reflect the communities they serve.

How school communities respond to and accept students with refugee and asylum-seeker backgrounds reflects something important about the school culture. If students' physical, cultural, academic and language differences lead educators to expect less of them, this is an indictment of the school culture. Such deficit thinking amounts to a subtle form of racism and its effects on students can last a lifetime. Principals must work to develop a shared understanding that intelligence comes in all types of skills and talents, dispositions and attitudes and teachers must diversify strategies to allow children to show what they know and can do. Widely used and restrictive western notions of intelligence, often predicated on a single norm-referenced test, fly in the face of this asset thinking. Children who have refugee and asylum-seeker backgrounds have great tenacity, resilience and capacity to survive – all strengths schools should value. Along with this asset-based mindset, educators need to reflect and implement effective pedagogical practices in the classroom, particularly around English instruction. These might include arts-based, cooking and gardening-focused approaches. Each may require more time than traditional instruction, but the results can be deeper and more positive. Creating school communities that effectively serve children and families with refugee and asylum-seeker backgrounds must start with a schoolwide belief in the capacity of these students and then a creative willingness to help these students grow.

## The PERMA model

Positive thinking, in addition to allowing improved cognition, motivation and creativity, is also believed to be critical for overall wellbeing; a vital part of the work of principals and their staff when supporting students with refugee and asylum-seeker experiences. Seligman, Ernst, Gillham, Reivich and Linkins (2009) and Seligman, Park and Peterson (2005) have investigated the power of positivity on wellbeing and happiness, while not neglecting what is already known about human suffering and disorders. Implementing a model based on five 'pillars' of wellbeing, Seligman and his colleagues have supported the work of educators seeking to integrate wellbeing into their everyday classroom interactions. Designed for regular cohorts of students, this model has much to offer principals and teachers supporting students with refugee and asylum-seeker experiences. Each of the components of the model have three characteristics in common: they can be measured independently of each other, are pursued for their own sakes and each contributes to overall wellbeing. This PERMA model comprises pillars dedicated to:

*Positive emotions*: This pillar may be the most difficult, but most important for students with refugee and asylum-seeker experiences. It demands a concentrated focus on actions and tasks that result in satisfaction, happiness, fulfilment and a sense of personal joy and accomplishment. It also involves developing a positive attitude and being optimistic about the past, present and the future. The difficulties here are apparent. However, it is important to recognise the model was developed with an acknowledgement of the suffering that may be endured by some individuals, to be cognisant of the impact of trauma and loss as discussed in Chapter 4 and to acknowledge the role of mindfulness and optimism in respect to the present and the future as opportunities for healing and increasingly autonomous action.

*Engagement*: This pillar indicates the importance of the type of deep engagement Csikszentmihalyi describes as 'flow'. Engaging in activities that have the appropriate degree of challenge and permit total absorption of positive emotion and attention is frequently demonstrated by individuals losing track of time, becoming oblivious to outside distractions and remaining totally in the current task. When engagement takes this form, neurotransmitters and hormones are released in the body that heighten feelings of wellbeing and facilitate the desire to engage in similar tasks on other occasions.

*Relationships*: These have been identified through several disciplinary lenses. Humans are designed to be social beings and strong positive relationships are critical to wellbeing and mental health. It appears that humans are 'hard-wired' to be social as neuroscientists can now identify that isolation and rejection transmit pain in the same areas of the brain as those associated with physical injury pain (see, for example, Prinstein, 2017; Slavich, 2020). These pain centres trigger responses to seek out social contact, especially in the context of loving and caring relationships. In Chapter 5, research indicated that the key to belonging in schools was the capacity to develop positive relationships with teachers, peers and other members of the school community. This is particularly crucial for students with refugee and asylum-seeker experiences as many of their previous positive relationships would have been undoubtedly destroyed or become unavailable to them as the result of their forced migration and their newcomer, refugee or asylum-seeker status in their new homelands. Belonging to a group, having positive relationships and social safety have been identified as human psychological needs that are foundational aspects of wellbeing for centuries.

*Meaning*: This pillar resonates with what scholars and philosophers have investigated for centuries: what is the meaning of life? To have reasons to survive, be resilient, to value work and other activities beyond what is required for basic needs is what Seligman and his colleagues identify as giving meaning to life. Some individuals find meaning in organised religions or spiritual practices, while others find it elsewhere in their everyday lives, their children and their families. This can be a particularly poignant wellbeing pillar for many refugees and asylum seekers who suffer from feelings of guilt or remorse as a consequence of surviving when other family or community members did not.

Students may also feel that they need to reproach themselves for the loss of siblings, parents and other close family members. Pedagogies, relationships and tasks that facilitate success and give meaning to their lives and hope for the future may be critical aspects of student wellbeing that can be instigated and maintained in educational contexts and are closely aligned with the final pillar of wellbeing.

*Achievement:* This pillar is of particular importance in schools where students are encouraged to develop personal, meaningful achievable learning goals (see, for example, Hansen & Wills, 2014; Kaplan & Maehr, 1999; Pintrich, 2000). The opportunity for students with refugee and asylum-seeker experiences to achieve their learning goals can afford them a safe space within which to negotiate their roles and identities in two cultures, invest in their relative strengths for strategising and help them prioritise their learning needs with some autonomy, a privilege which could rarely be afforded to these students in their displacement, their journeys and perhaps even in their past learning experiences. Principals have opportunities to facilitate meaningful achievement as a pillar of wellbeing for these and other students in their school communities.

### Research findings

Many of the principals we interviewed spoke about the power of positivity and how a supportive culture builds upon itself. Two leaders who offered important observations were a high school principal in Australia and a primary principal in the United States.

> Context: I have been a principal in secondary schools (Years 7–12) for the last 20 years. My school has roughly 1,000 students and is in a regional area. I had 60 refugee students in total that came through with me, all with various levels of visas and various levels of support. Many of them we didn't know their ages. I hired an ex-primary school principal who learned Farsi and actually spoke to them in their own language. The boys were all Muslim and really we are a school which is not very religious in any way, in manner or form.

> *One of the teachers I had was teaching them all to drive. And I said to him, "You really have to be really careful," he has a BMW and they were driving his BMW on their learner licence. And he said, "It's okay, they haven't got a father, so I'm their father." It's all about having that support. And then they blossom. Refugee students blossom and grow, and they want to do more and more, and they want to be part of something that acknowledges them as people… I maintain contact with those young people. We had – one of my boys became engaged and the boys came from Brisbane, Melbourne and Sydney about, two months ago and all got together. So, they remember their education.*

> Context: We are a diverse elementary school (K-5). The largest population are Hispanic students; after that, it is students from the Middle East

speaking Pashto, Farsi, those students from Iraq, Afghanistan, Pakistan, and then other students from different countries in Africa. A large majority of my students are English as a Second Language (ESOL) and we have 12 ESOL teachers and two paraprofessionals.

*One of the things, I think, is the more teachers get on board, the more it helps. So, we had this one teacher who just thought, if you did not speak English, you did not belong... And I tried, I tried, and when it was just me trying to change their mind, I was not making any progress. But the more teachers that I got on board to be working with these kids and excited to be working with these kids, and the more other teachers were making progress and their kids were making academic growth, and they were getting all excited, the more he realised this school just was not the right fit for him, and so he eventually left... I think the more I get excited, then my kids get excited and have academic growth. Then, the other teachers are getting excited and these teachers are having growth and your circle is getting bigger and bigger and bigger. Some of those teachers who just do not want to have that mindset are either going to jump on board or jump ship.*

### Unique contexts, global principles

Our Australian high school principal pushed her staff to form relationships with students, to give students skills beyond academics and to provide someone who places confidence in them. The teacher who took it upon himself to show his students how to drive demonstrated commitment and offered an opportunity for them to achieve. This principal keenly observed that students with refugee and asylum-seeker experiences blossom and grow and seek greater opportunities when valued and acknowledged as individuals. The holistic approach she employs to supporting student wellbeing and fostering growth has yielded close, lasting relationships as evidenced by the wedding described. Our principal from the United States offers insight into dealing with staff members who do not support the school vision. A passionate leader, she worked hard to bring all her teachers along to her vision through her energy and excitement. Over time and by experiencing student success, the critical mass supporting her vision grew. But, with the recalcitrant teacher, she engaged in numerous didactic conversations until it became evident he needed to leave the school. This principal is clear her teachers need to embrace the school's positive approach to refugee and asylum-seeker students or they need to find other places to work.

Creating schools with a positive ethos is vitally important work for principals. Being positive helps students with refugee and asylum-seeker backgrounds achieve, it gives them positive emotions, helps them to make strong social relationships, gives meaning to what they are doing, and it assists them to integrate. Students need support and opportunities to achieve as success builds on success and, with the right types of support, students can overcome the negative effects of trauma. For principals, developing a team of educators who are willing to participate in the necessary hard work of supporting these students, can be challenging. As our leader in the United States demonstrated, principals must be willing to engage in the difficult conversations individually with teachers who have not embraced the school's positive vision and to counsel them to either get on board or move on. Principals also must recognise teachers for having a positive effect on students, for fuelling their sense of belonging and developing all their capacities. This work is not just about student cognition; it is about the importance of being well before learning can take place. Principals who craft and promote a school vision based on fostering wellbeing and achievement, who support staff members and who purposefully address detractors, can build an environment that truly supports students with refugee and asylum-seeker experiences.

## Chapter conclusion

There is a widely used expression that experts make their work look easy. Certainly, the principals profiled in this chapter could appear to make the work of positive leadership look easy. It is not. The deliberate, purposeful journey to integrate students with refugee and asylum-seeking backgrounds into the fabric of a caring, compassionate school culture built on success for all is a daily work in progress. Many newly arrived students have unresolved issues that can manifest themselves in inappropriate or unexpected behaviours. Some reeling from trauma require extra special interventions. Some families struggle with the cultural differences of how children are treated in their new countries. A caring principal with consistently positive approaches can build, over time, a school culture to evolve to a common understanding of what it takes to be a learning community. The connections between positive leadership and the imperative of engaging pedagogy is explored in Chapter 8.

## References

Alford, J. H. (2014). "Well, hang on, they're actually much better than that!": Disrupting dominant discourses of deficit about English language learners in senior high school English. *English Teaching: Practice & Critique (University of Waikato)*, 13(3), 71–88. https://files.eric.ed.gov/fulltext/EJ1050176.pdf.

Bandura, A. (1986). *Self efficacy beliefs in human functioning.* www.uky.edu/~eushe2/Paja res/effpassages.html.

Blackwell, D., & Melzak, S. (2000). *Far from the Battle but Still at War: Troubled Refugee Children in School.* Child Psychotherapy Trust.

Csikszentmihalyi, M. (1988). The flow experience and its significance for human psychology. In M. Csikszentmihalyi & S. Csikszentmihalyi (Eds.), *Optimal Experience: Psychological Studies of Flow in Consciousness* (pp. 3–37). Cambridge University Press.

Csikszentmihalyi, M. (1991a). Consciousness for the twenty-first century. *Zygon*, 26(1), 7–25.

Csikszentmihalyi, M. (1991b). Work as flow. In *Flow: The Psychology of Optimal Experience* (pp. 143–163). New York: Harper & Row.

Csikszentmihalyi, M., & Lebuda, I. (2017). A window into the bright side of psychology: Interview with Mihaly Csikszentmihalyi. *Europe's Journal of Psychology*, 13(4), 810–821. doi:10.5964/ejop.v13i4.1482.

Dupré, J., & O'Neill, J. (1998). Against reductionist explanations of human behaviour. *Proceedings of the Aristotelian Society, Supplementary Volumes*, 72, 153–171, 173–188.

Dweck, C. (2006). *Mindset*. Random House.

Frater-Mathieson, K. (2004). Refugee trauma, loss and grief: Implications for intervention. In R. Hamilton & D. Moore (Eds.), *Educational Interventions for Refugee Children* (pp. 12–34). Routledge.

Fredrickson, B. (2000). Cultivating positive emotions to optimize health and well-being. *Prevention and Treatment*, 3. www.wisebrain.org/papers/CultPosEmot.pdf.

Fredrickson, B. (2001). The role of positive emotions in positive psychology. *American Psychologist*, 56(3), 218–226.

Gardner, H. (1983). *Frames of Mind* (1st ed.). William Heinemann Ltd.

Hansen, B. D., & Wills, H. P. (2014). The effects of goal setting, contingent reward, and instruction on writing skills. *Journal of Applied Behavior Analysis*, 47(1), 171–175. doi:10.1002/jaba.92.

Horn, J., & Cattell, R. (1967). Age differences in fluid and crystallized intelligence. *Acta Psychologica*, 26, 107–129.

Kaplan, A., & Maehr, M. L. (1999). Enhancing the motivation of African American students: An achievement goal theory perspective. *The Journal of Negro Education*, 68(1), 23–41.

MacLure, M., Jones, L., Holmes, R., & MacRae, C. (2012). Becoming a problem: Behaviour and reputation in the early years classroom. *British Educational Research Journal*, 38(3), 447–471. doi:10.1080/01411926.2011.552709.

McMichael, C., Gifford, S. M., & Correa-Velez, I. (2011). Negotiating family, navigating resettlement: Family connectedness amongst resettled youth with refugee backgrounds living in Melbourne, Australia. *Journal of Youth Studies*, 14(2), 179–195. doi:10.1080/13676261.2010.506529.

Mthethwa-Sommers, S., & Kisiara, O. (2015). Listening to students from refugee backgrounds: Lessons for education professionals. *Perspectives on Urban Education*, 12(1). https://files.eric.ed.gov/fulltext/EJ1056671.pdf.

Pintrich, P. (2000). The role of goal orientation in self-regulated learning. In M. Boekaerts (Ed.), *Handbook of Self-Regulated Learning* (pp. 452–494). Academic Press.

Prinstein, M. (2017). *Popular: The Power of Likeability in a Status-Obsessed World*. Viking.

Rutter, J., & Jones, C. (Eds.). (1998). *Refugee Education: Mapping the Field*. Stylus Publishing.

Seligman, M., Ernst, R., Gillham, J., Reivich, K., & Linkins, M. (2009). Positive education: Positive psychology and classroom interventions. *Oxford Review of Education*, 35(3), 293–311.

Seligman, M., Park, N., & Peterson, C. (2005). Positive psychology progress: Empirical validation of interventions. *American Psychologist*, 60(5), 410–421.

Sellars, M. (2017). *Reflective Practice for Teachers*. Sage.

Slavich, G. (2020). Social safety theory: A biologically based evolutionary perspective on life stress, health, and behavior. *Annual Review of Clinical Psychology*, 16, 265–295. doi:10.1146/annurev-clinpsy-032816-045159.

Spearman, C. (1904). General intelligence: Objectively determined and measured. *American Journal of Psychology*, 15(2), 201–292.

Sternberg, R., & Kaufman, A. S. (1998). Human abilities. *Annual Review of Psychology*, 49(1), 479–502.

Thurstone, L. (1938). *Primary Mental Abilities*. University of Chicago Press.

Uptin, J., Wright, J., & Harwood, V. (2016). Finding education: Stories of how young former refugees constituted strategic identities in order to access school. *Race Ethnicity and Education*, 19(3), 598–617. doi:10.1080/13613324.2014.885428.

# 8    Supportive pedagogical approaches

## Introduction

Pedagogy is a broad term that encompasses the teaching and learning that takes place in a school. It reflects the way school leaders and their educators envision the learning journey, and it encompasses the philosophies, methods and values of the interactions between teachers and students. For students with refugee and asylum-seeker experiences, progressive and supportive pedagogies, for example, project-based learning, gardening, art making, cooking, music and drama experiences, can offer a vital lifeline for their success in their new homes. Conversely, traditional pedagogies may not provide the kind of support nor facilitate the positive culture that was discussed in Chapter 7. This chapter presents research on supportive, expressive and transformational pedagogies and the need for teachers who believe in such approaches. Insights from global educators who understand the opportunity of pedagogy to create places of belonging are offered.

## Supportive pedagogies

There are numerous approaches to teaching and learning, each with its own particular strength and limitations, variations and applications. These can be broadly categorised into three categories, which overlap to inform and enrich each other (Cummins, 2000, 2009; Wink, 2011). The most traditional, economical and time-efficient group of pedagogical strategies are those such as direct instruction, explicit teaching and transmission. All of these are teacher directed and are typically 'one-size-fits-all' instruction, irrespective of student diversity, capabilities, readiness, interests or learning preferences. While these pedagogical strategies are important for students with refugee and asylum-seeker backgrounds to learn explicit, non-negotiable facts such as letter and number names and symbols, they are not ideal for newcomer students (Taylor, 2008). When these cohorts of students are placed in educational contexts that reflect their chronological age, these pedagogical strategies disempower students and place them as 'deficit' in comparison to their classmates who have typically not had significantly interrupted schooling, displacement and developmental

DOI: 10.4324/9781003090731-8

trauma cognitive impact and are hopefully not as emotionally or mentally vulnerable (De Bellis, 2005, 2010). This is not to disregard the very real needs of other students in the school, but the additional barriers of language learning and culture swapping to meet the demands of educational norms and customs in their new homelands can be exacerbated by the stress of well-meaning, but inappropriate, pedagogical strategies implemented to learn about content about which they have no prior knowledge or experiences (Dryden-Peterson et al., 2019; Hattam & Every, 2010; Keddie, 2012; Matthews, 2008; Pinson & Arnot, 2007).

The second group of strategies are reflected in transactional pedagogical practices, also known as the generative model of learning (Wink, 2011), in which students are not required to be passive recipients of information, but to engage in the process personally. These pedagogical strategies facilitate the social constructivist theories of Piaget and Vygotsky (Sellars, 2017) and can readily support the learning of students with refugee and asylum-seeker backgrounds. A typical implementation using these strategies is collaborative learning in small groups. These can be developed to ensure that the content is within the experiences of all the students; and to ensure these experiences are shared, these pedagogies are frequently supported by field trips, outings and incursions, facilitating a common experience from which to develop individual knowledge and conceptual skills. It is possible also that these groups provide an ideal opportunity for teachers to practise the basic letter and number names and symbols which are necessary for any written expression. In this way, the three groups of pedagogies can be observed to be on a continuum; from as little as possible transmission to the social-emotional and linguistic support of constructivism, which reflects the students' own active participation based on common experiences and then progressively moves to totally student-orientated strategies of transformative pedagogies. The critical aspect of the potential of students with refugee and asylum-seeker backgrounds is that the aforementioned impact of the diverse and complex trauma they have experienced means that they are not mentally or emotionally prepared to undertake learning in either transmission or transactional classrooms.

The experiences of students with refugee and asylum-seeker experiences are not common to the other class members. Additionally, the code switching (Samway et al., 2020) and culture switching with which these student groups must engage to follow orally presented instruction in a second or additional language typically results in cognitive overload (de Jong, 2010), which is neither helpful nor productive. It is because of all these factors that the most productive, sensitive and appropriate pedagogical approach for these students, at least initially, is that of transformative pedagogy. This pedagogical model allows students to engage with learning as therapy and, as will be discussed later, is frequently in learning contexts that facilitate self-expression, orally, visually or by other means, and accommodate the development of conversational and other informal language skills.

## Research findings

Many of the school leaders we interviewed commented on the importance of rethinking pedagogical approaches for students with refugee and asylum-seeker experiences. Two leaders who stood out in this regard were a primary principal in Australia and a high school principal in Australia.

> Context: Our school is kindergarten to Year 6 with roughly 160 students. There was about three and a half years where every new-arrival primary school student that had just moved to the district started in this school. Although that kind of changed when the Syrian cohort started coming through; they started going to other primary schools at that time. In the past, we had close to 50% refugee students who were newly arrived at any one point in time, but now I'm probably more about 15 or 20% students from a culturally/linguistically diverse background.

> *There are different pedagogies that will raise the status of children in their classrooms and when you're looking at that and staff are looking at that, they start to go, "okay, when I select these activities, is this giving a place for these students to be valued and to shine?" Because then when a student's status begins to rise, that in turn influences the way that they belong, the way that they feel accepted. When they produce mastery experiences, it improves their self-efficacy. They find their place within the world and within the school... I've now employed a specialist teacher who had a background in Visual Arts. We have used art as a way to actually explore what we were doing in terms of learning English language. To a certain degree there was a therapeutic nature to that approach that allowed them this sense of self-expression. It allowed them a voice when they didn't necessarily have the English language to have a voice. It allowed us to value their work in a different way, because of the nature of the drawings, their artistic mark making. It was a whole range of things that allowed for this affirmation of who they were and their experiences.*

> Context: I've been a principal in secondary schools for the last 20 years. My school has around 1,100 students (Years 7–12). We are located on the outskirts of a regional centre. I have had about 60 refugee students come through the school, with varying levels of visa and English levels.

> *The people who worked with the students are very proud of how they've succeeded. I think what those teachers had in common was that they were very people centred; that they were teachers who obviously put students first. They weren't as rigid, they were more flexible, and they were quite willing to be empathetic. We do have teachers who aren't in that category who want to teach by the book and who are very good at their craft but aren't student-oriented. It's about building the relationships. You pick the teacher who you know will build strong relations. The kids all know, because when you put out your subjects, they gravitate towards those teachers and*

*they are where all the numbers are; you know that the kids are very wise, and they know which teachers are student-orientated. It's not the song that the kids choose when they're in high school. It's the singer. I know who those people are. And we know who they are. They're invaluable.*

### Unique contexts, global principles

Each of our principals was concerned with providing students with refugee and asylum-seeker backgrounds with opportunities and environments for success. Our Australian primary principal developed and staffed an innovative pedagogical arts-based program that enabled his students to visually share their experiences and feelings. In addition to being therapeutic, the program allowed students to work in their own language and the host language and it gave them a voice and status in the school. This principal operates on the premise that giving students forums in which to shine raises their visibility within the school and improves their self-efficacy and wellbeing. More importantly, he has created a school culture in which his teachers analyse their curriculum and pedagogy to ensure students with refugee and asylum-seeker backgrounds have ample opportunities for success. Our Australian high school principal places great emphasis on hiring the right teachers with the right dispositions as she believes student/teacher relationships trump other factors. While she respects skilled teachers who are technically sound, she places little emphasis on this in the hiring process. This principal looks for flexibility, empathy and people-centred teachers as she believes they genuinely take pride in the successes of their students and the students appreciate these teachers. Importantly, both leaders recognise the need for well-trained, caring teachers to successfully implement supportive pedagogies.

Students who have suffered great trauma, who find themselves in completely foreign environments and are attempting to navigate two cultures, are likely to suffer self-doubt and wellbeing issues. Principals and teachers must work collectively to develop and offer opportunities to these students to be successful. Educators should embrace supportive pedagogies that respect the first languages of children with refugee and asylum-seeker backgrounds. Art, cooking and gardening programs each offer a therapeutic outlet and ways for all children to demonstrate skills, gain recognition and develop self-confidence. By implementing such programs and celebrating all students, principals can send a message to the school community that all types of accomplishments are valued. As with so many other components of effective schools, the success of these efforts will boil down to the quality and dispositions of the teachers staffing the individual classrooms. Educators who connect with students on a personal level, who care about their success as individuals, are willing to rethink their classroom practices to develop opportunities for students to shine. As our Australian principal advised, these are the teachers with whom principals want to fill their schools.

## Expressive pedagogies

Engaging with arts-based pedagogies and content has proven to be successful with students with refugee and asylum-seeker experiences. It appears to have many benefits for this cohort in particular, who need flexible, differentiated curriculum and pedagogies in their resettlement school contexts in order to thrive and be included (Carlton, 2015; Correa-Velez et al., 2010; Sorgen, 2015). Arts-based curriculums lend themselves more readily to personal interpretation, cultural expression and opportunities to express feelings and heal trauma. Additionally, music, art, dance and drama are the keystones of community identity in many traditional cultures. The neurological impact on the brain that engaging in dance activities produces is not limited to sensations of physical enjoyment; it stimulates growth and production of brain cells, improving the connectivity between both sides of the brain, cognition and spatial awareness (Brown & Parsons, 2008; Dale et al., 2007; Hanna, 2015). Music and singing are both pivotal supporting activities in the learning of a new language and have therapeutic benefits for participants, including students with refugee and asylum-seeker experiences (Fonseca-Mora et al., 2015; Ludke et al., 2014; Moreno et al., 2015). Baker and Jones (2006) also reported that newly arrived students with refugee experiences in their study were better able to control their sadness, anxiety and aggressive classroom behaviours as the result of engaging with a wide range of music-based activities, which may indicate that music and related activities have an important role to play in the development of the executive function cognitive capacities which are frequently delayed or inhibited by developmental trauma (De Bellis, 2010).

Other arts-based activities have been observed to support the learning and healing of students with refugee and asylum-seeker experiences (Samway et al., 2020). Balfour et al. (2015) supported students emotionally and mentally by engaging them with theatre and inviting dramatic and writing activities, which helped them express their concerns, their sadness and other impacts of forced displacement and migratory difficulties, concluding that they became more resilient and optimistic about developing new lives as the result of resettlement. Bunyan et al. (2003, p. 62) sum up the importance of this type of activity, especially for students who come from backgrounds of oracy. They state:

> When acting in role as someone else, somewhere else, pupils look at their lives, identities, values and cultures in a place where their real status and identity are not at stake. Drama is part of our basic human need to symbolise the world through the conscious application of form to meaning in ways that engage the intellect and the emotions. Through drama pupils can develop their 'emotional literacy' and analytical awareness through seeing the world from other perspectives. The imaginative engagement underpins the development of their critical thinking and writing.

The work of Sonn et al. (2013) echoed these sentiments as part of their arts-based intervention which engaged students with refugee and asylum-seeker experiences as vocal participants. They captured the voices of these students as part of their data collection, indicating that their findings challenged the stereotypical view of these cohorts of students as deeply traumatised, sad and depressed. It may be thanks to the intervention activities that they implemented with these students that the students developed greater capacities to engage socially, relate to significant others and become more positive about their prospects. While not strictly arts based, Arizpe et al. (2014) used visual texts to improve the literacy skills of newcomer students in primary schools, finding that the generative theme approach of Freire supported the students' appreciation of intercultural literacy and understandings. Hope (2008, 2011) used children's literature as an educative tool with which to integrate students into schools and build connections between them and the other students, facilitating the development of self-identity in their new environments. Wellman and Bey (2015), also understanding the wealth of opportunities that arts-based programs and pedagogies provided for students with refugee and asylum-seeker experiences to improve their levels of wellbeing, sense of autonomy and inclusion into secondary schools, included specific pedagogical training around these possibilities for preservice art teachers in their secondary programs.

### Research findings

Several principals with whom we spoke had implemented arts-based programs in their schools to support children with refugee and asylum-seeker experiences. Two who stood out included a primary principal in Australia and a primary principal in Northern Ireland.

> Context: I started off in high schools (Years 7–12), then later became a behaviour consultant and now I am a primary school principal (K-6). My previous school was around 45% refugee students, but the school I now work at has around 15% students from a linguistically diverse background. I try to hire teachers to match the diversity of my school.

> *I looked at what the research says, how it takes 8 years to learn formal English, and up to 13 years if you've got trauma experiences in your background. I decided to employ an art teacher to work on the students' English. So, we did activities from, "can you pass me the red pencil?" as we learn colours; to talking and singing; and we used art to assess content. There's a whole range of things. The teachers drew pictures for the kids to try and guess what the picture was and so it was a whole range of language, descriptive language. Amazing things happen in that context. The students also drew, which meant that we started putting on art shows at a commercial gallery. Then the paintings were sold, of all these amazing drawings. There was one boy who drew mountain tops and explained to us the strategies that the Taliban use. It's this way that they were able to draw it and express it and to get it out. It has a therapeutic nature which allows them to have some self-expression. That allowed them a voice, when they didn't necessarily have the English*

*language to have a voice. So, that was an approach that we used, that was probably vastly different to the way a lot of schools approach it. We did other things, we had drumming; however, I am Drumbeat trained, but it was not appropriate for me to run drumming in that situation. I found a guy who is a worldwide, acknowledged master from West Senegal in drum and dance, and so I employed him to come in and he ran all those sorts of things.*

Context: My school demographic has changed since 2010. My school is in a capital city and was built in the early twentieth century to serve the local community, but we are now around 80% English as an additional dialect. Part of the complexity of our school is we are in a rich postcode but the students at our school aren't affluent. To begin with we had no idea about refugees or asylum seekers; we had to learn along the way.

*What we're doing is, we are dealing with children who have Attachment Disorder. This may be due to whatever trauma they have had. One of our teachers is fully trained in Nurture [practices] so he will do a lot of things like Play Therapy, Lego Therapy, and Drawing and Talking Therapy. He is currently seeking some coun-selling experience as well. He's an absolutely wonderful teacher; really good with behaviour. He is really good at dealing with [children's] adverse experiences. We can see that the children really thrive, and we can see a [huge] difference when those children come back into class.*

### Unique contexts, global principles

Though they are working on opposite sides of the planet in very different contexts, each of our principals shared very similar observations about the power and promise of arts-based education for children with refugee and asylum-seeker backgrounds. Our Australian primary principal implemented a visual arts program that culminated in students exhibiting and selling their works to the general public. The actual act of art making was meaningful for these students as it allowed them to share their experiences and demonstrate what they know, and the process allowed these students to be autonomous. This principal also implemented a rich drumming program in his school. Though he is a trained musician, this principal recognised that he was not the right person to lead such an effort and he brought in a Senegalese instructor. Our Northern Irish primary principal has implemented a variety of creative therapy programs as it is important to find experiences that resonate with individual students. Engaging students in building, drawing, drama and then encouraging them to talk about the work is key to its success. These are not routine programs that one would find in most schools; rather, these are pro-grams the principal and her team have identified as valuable. This principal has placed much trust and autonomy in the teacher leading these initiatives, a signal to her entire staff that she supports programs and people working beyond the norm to support children with refugee and asylum-seeker backgrounds.

Expressive pedagogies offer a host of benefits for schools that are working to support children with refugee and asylum-seeker backgrounds. Developing self-confidence, autonomy and wellbeing as well as language acquisition and academic gains are outcomes of such approaches. While jumping into a traditional western curriculum might be daunting and place newly arrived students at a disadvantage, a non-traditional art or drumming program can level the playing field and help these students shine. These experiences also break up the traditional school day, a schedule that students may not be ready to follow. Offering diverse opportunities is also important as each student needs to have a chance to find his or her passions. Principals must be aware that most of these pedagogical strategies take time and a huge amount of effort in order to see gains. The work is valuable but requires sustained commitment and dedicated personnel. As each of our leaders demonstrate, it is vital to look inside and outside of the school for necessary expertise to develop, implement and sustain these important programs.

## Transformative pedagogies

The very supportive arts-based program and pedagogies discussed above were typically interactive, transactional and socio-constructive in nature. Depending on the incidents of explicit teaching, where the teacher takes on the role of the transmitter of knowledge, the pedagogical approaches in arts-based programs are co-constructed by the student as an active participant in the learning. In these mid-continuum teaching and learning contexts, teachers' roles change, and they become the facilitators of student knowledge. At the opposite end of the continuum from the transmission pedagogies, there are strategies by which teachers mentor the students, following their interests and providing guidance that is not necessarily transmissive (Sellars, 2017). These are the totally student-centred transformational pedagogies. The activities and products that are the result of this learning are reflective of the students' own investigations and interpretations of areas that engage and motivate them to be independent learners. The focus of transformative pedagogical practices is not only to transform the students' learning experiences in formal educational contexts, but to develop critical thinking in relation to notions of social justice, challenging racism and other areas of injustice and inequity in education and transforming identity through education (see, for example, Ahana, 2014; Bell, 2016; Brisco, 2013; Gardner & Kelly, 2008; Haber-Curran & Tillapaugh, 2015; Illeris, 2014; Levitt, 2008; Nagda et al., 2003; Onsando & Billett, 2014).

While much is written about the potential of transformative pedagogical practices for all students in the tradition of Pestalozzi, Froebel and other early European educators who trusted students to engage themselves in their interests and to be naturally investigative and curious (Allen, 2017; Gravil, 1997; Horlacher, 2011), much of this pedagogical approach is now confined to specialist preschool settings which have not been totally influenced by the neoliberal impact on the purpose of education (Sellars & Imig, 2020). Students in school are more typically exposed to transmission pedagogies validated by account-abilities, efficiencies and economies of ontology and epistemology, neglecting the imperative to educate for democracy, social justice and responsible global citizenship (Sellars, 2020). In adult education, there has been considerable interest in Mezirow's (1981, 1991, 1998, 2003) notion of critical reflection in education, which is focused on examining and questioning the very basis of what individuals value, feel and operationalise, the ways in which they do this and the reasons that underpin the engagement with the critical reflection process on a personal level.

> In 1991, Mezirow collapsed these levels into three dimensions of reflection including content (reflecting on what we perceive, think, feel, and act), process (reflecting on how we perform the functions of perceiving), and "premise reflection" [which] involves becoming aware of the why we perceive, think, feel or act as we do.
>
> (Mezirow, 1991, p. 108 in Taylor, 2017, pp. 78–79).

Much of the purpose of transformative pedagogical perspectives are focused on problem-based learning, and most recently, identifying and examining the process of problem finding before the event. O'Sullivan (1999, 2008; O'Sullivan et al., 2002) also comments on the need for critical reflection as the basis of transformative pedagogies, especially in the context of human existence as part of an entire biosphere. He highlights five major areas that are required to effect a change in educational consciousness (2008, pp. xv–xvi). These are holism, the web of life, wisdom of women, wisdom of indigenous peoples and spirituality. While it is not possible to extrapolate these central components here, a more detailed investigation would reflect the concerns of many school leaders and their communities. The ultimate goal of all transformative pedagogical approaches is to reach from classrooms to communities with the purpose of changing society; transforming it to become more democratic, more equitable and more sustainable for all communities, but especially for those who remain disempowered. It is within the reach of school leaders to instigate these pedagogies into their classrooms.

### Research findings

School leaders we interviewed highlighted the benefits of transformative pedagogies for their students with refugee and asylum-seeker experiences. A high school principal in the United States and a primary principal in New Zealand offered pertinent observations.

> Context: I am the proud principal of a high school (Grades 9–12) that is less than 10 years old. I was undocumented growing up and I came to the US when I was five years old; I feel like that's where I draw a lot of what we do in our school. Over 60% of our students have been in the country two years or less and 100% of our school are English-language learners.

*I really believe that a lot of the decision-making around schooling has not focused on students whatsoever and much more around adult behaviours and adult egos, their needs. One of the things that we believe in is positive youth development and understanding that all decisions that we make, everything that happens in our school building, are centred on students. For example, when we do hiring, our students are ultimately the ones that decide which teachers come into our building. We know that we're putting in front of them two high-quality finalists, and whichever one they go with, we would work okay with. Just the approach and how we do things, we do group teacher interviews. So, for the first four years, as we were hiring, we put together an entire process that was different from others. Mainly because we wanted to see different facets of what the prospective teachers could do in our school building.*

Context: I'm the principal at a primary school in New Zealand, from Year 1 to 8 (ages 5–13). We are quite a large school for the area, with around 520 children. We are quite diverse, in the sense that we are diverse in terms of culture, but we also say diverse in terms of background and socioeconomics. When I say diverse culturally, we have 20 different cultures here but not lots of some of those individual cultures.

*A lot of what we do is influenced by New Zealand's government pushing the curriculum. Particularly in education it is very much about, "we've got a whole lot of kids that are not succeeding in a system. What do we have to do to change that? And is this working with these people?" The government has tried to turn that around; they realised, "actually, we've been getting it wrong. What can we do now to try and make it better for everybody?" It's like anything, you could talk about something as a vision, but if people don't understand what that looks like in practice, it won't work. Which, I think, is half the problem. I do think it's about everyone has a culture, regardless of the fact you might be white, middle class or whatever, we have a culture. If you want to work with people you need to know what's important to them. You want to bring the best out of people? You need to know what's important to them... We are not too scared to say, "hey in your culture, what do you do about this? Or, can you tell us how you do it?" We invite that sharing, always. They love to tell us, the kids love to tell us, and the parent loves to come and show us. So, we are quite invitational in that sense.*

### Unique contexts, global principles

Each of our principals were concerned with giving their students a real voice in the operation of the school and a role in their own educational journey. For our high school principal from the United States, one way this empowerment takes form is allowing students to make school hiring decisions. While atypical, the strategy gives students a powerful sense of ownership. This principal, who experienced the trauma of being an undocumented resident, holds the perspective that schools are not designed to meet the needs of students; rather, they are built around the needs of the adult stakeholders. Verbalising this to his school community has flipped the conversation and put students at the centre of decision-making. Our primary principal from New Zealand operates from the understanding that every member of the school community has a culture that is important to them. This principal encourages his staff to find out what is important to each student and then use that information to shape learning. He has created a school culture where teachers engage in continuous dialogue with students and invite families to share and be part of the curriculum. Through their purposeful action, both principals have developed democratic places of learning.

Systemic demands, accountability pressures and conservative notions of schooling can often create schools that do not prioritise the children they serve. Such places can be especially detrimental to students who come from refugee and asylum-seeker backgrounds. Our two principals have strong ideas about the need to share school responsibilities with students, share cultures, share backgrounds and share experiences. This sharing is transformative pedagogy, and it is ultimately about empowering and changing society's perception of these students. In classrooms that have always been orientated towards western culture and western students, the act of giving newly arrived students a voice and incorporating their ideas and experiences can enrich the educational experience of all students. It takes strong leaders to rethink system policies as our leader in the United States did or to place students' diverse cultures at the centre of the school curriculum as our principal in New Zealand has done. While some countries and school systems are certainly more welcoming, inclusive and accommodating than others, it is ultimately up to the principal to initiate and support programs at the school level.

## Chapter conclusion

Supportive and responsive pedagogy is at the heart of caring, compassionate learner-focused schools. Students with refugee and asylum-seeker experiences, living with trauma, adjusting to drastically new lifestyles and culture, a new language and new social contexts, must be offered diverse opportunities to shine in their new school. For schools that have long been on the journey of supporting the talents of individuals, embedding newly arrived students with different backgrounds is less challenging than for schools where transactional and direct instruction approaches govern the culture of the learning environment. While English acquisition and core content are vital, principals must lead with the heart and support student wellbeing first. The principal's role in creating the pedagogical freedom to centre the learning on each child is key to facilitating acceptance of the processes of care, love, hope and learning that make a school special. In this chapter, reflective principals shared their journeys of recognising, integrating and learning from newly arrived students. This process of deep reflection is the core of this book and is the capacity that can make or break a principal's vision of success for all. The importance of developing a supportive school community that is responsive and welcoming to all stakeholders and the role of the principal in this work are explored in Chapter 9.

# References

Ahana, K. (2014). A new era of critical thinking in professional programs. *Transformative Dialogues: Teaching & Learning Journal*, 7(3), 1–9.

Allen, A. (2017). Pestalozzi, Fröbel, and the origins of the kindergarten. In A. Allen (Ed.), *The Transatlantic Kindergarten: Education and Women's Movements in Germany and the United States*. Oxford Scholarship Online. doi:10.1093/acprof:oso/9780190274412.001.0001.

Arizpe, E., Bagelman, C., Devlin, A. M., Farrell, M., & McAdam, J. E. (2014). Visualizing intercultural literacy: Engaging critically with diversity and migration in the classroom through an image-based approach. *Language and Intercultural Communication*, 14(3), 304–321. doi:10.1080/14708477.2014.903056.

Baker, F., & Jones, C. (2006). The effect of music therapy services on classroom behaviours of newly arrived refugee students in Australia—a pilot study. *Emotional and Behavioural Difficulties*, 11(4), 249–260. doi:10.1080/13632750601022170.

Balfour, M., Bundy, P., Burton, B., Dunn, J., & Woodrow, N. (2015). *Resettlement: Drama, Refugees and Resilience* (M. Balfour & S. Preston, Eds.). Bloomsbury.

Bell, D. V. J. (2016). Twenty-first century education: Transformative education for sustainability and responsible citizenship. *Journal of Teacher Education for Sustainability*, 18(1), 48–56. doi:10.1515/jtes-2016-0004.

Brisco, P. (2013). Developing transformative leaders to support everyday antiracism practices. *Canadian Journal of Educational Administration and Policy*, 142, 134–159.

Brown, S., & Parsons, L. (2008). The neuroscience of dance. *Scientific American*, 299, 78–83.

Bunyan, P., Donelan, K., & Moore, R. (2003). Writing in the sand: Drama, oracy and writing in the middle years. *Literacy Learning: The Middle Years*, 11(2), 61–64.

Carlton, S. (2015). Reprint of: Connecting, belonging: Volunteering, wellbeing and leadership among refugee youth. *International Journal of Disaster Risk Reduction, 14*(2), 160–167. doi:10.1016/j.ijdrr.2015.10.010.

Correa-Velez, I., Gifford, S. M., & Barnett, A. G. (2010). Longing to belong: Social inclusion and wellbeing among youth with refugee backgrounds in the first three years in Melbourne, Australia. *Social Science and Medicine*, 71(8), 1399–1408. doi:10.1016/j.socscimed.2010.07.018.

Cummins, J. (2000). 'This place nurtures my spirit': Creating contexts of empowerment in linguistically-diverse schools. In R. Phillipson (Ed.), *Rights to Language: Equity, Power, and Education* (pp. 249–258). Lawrence Erlbaum Associates, Inc.

Cummins, J. (2009). Transformative multiliteracies pedagogy: School-based strategies for closing the achievement gap. *Multiple Voices for Ethnically Diverse Exceptional Learners*, 11(2), 38–56.

Dale, J., Hyatt, J., & Hollerman, J. (2007). The neuroscience of dance and the dance of neuroscience: Defining a path of inquiry. *The Journal of Aesthetic Education*, 41(3), 89–110.

De Bellis, M. (2010). Developmental traumatology: A commentary on the factors for risk and resiliency in the case of an adolescent Javanese Boy. In C. Worthman, P. Plotsky, D. Schechter, & C. Cummings (Eds.), *Formative Experiences: The Interaction of Caring, Culture and Developmental Psychobiology*. Cambridge University Press.

De Bellis, M. (2005). The psychobiology of neglect. *Child Maltreatment*, 10(2), 150–172. doi:10.1177/1077559505275116.

de Jong, T. (2010). Cognitive load theory, educational research, and instructional design: Some food for thought. *Instructional Science*, 38, 105–134.

Dryden-Peterson, S., Adelman, E., Bellino, M., & Chopra, V. (2019). The purposes of refugee education: Policy and practice of including refugees in national education systems. *Sociology of Education*, 92(4). doi:10.1177/0038040719863054.

Fonseca-Mora, M. C., Jara-Jiménez, P., & Gómez-Domínguez, M. (2015). Musical plus phonological input for young foreign language readers. *Frontiers in Psychology*, 6, 1–9. doi:10.3389/fpsyg.2015.00286.

Gardner, M., & Kelly, U. (Eds.). (2008). *Narrating Transformative Learning in Education*. Macmillan.

Gravil, R. (1997). "Knowledge not purchased with the loss of power": Wordsworth, Pestalozzi and the "spots of time". *European Romantic Review*, 8(3), 231–261. doi:10.1080/10509585.1997.12029228.

Haber-Curran, P., & Tillapaugh, D. W. (2015). Student-centered transformative learning in leadership education: An examination of the teaching and learning process. *Journal of Transformative Education*, 13(1), 65–84. doi:10.1177/1541344614559947.

Hanna, J. (2015). Need smarts? Just dance. Dancing boosts brain cells and their connections for lifelong learning. *Teachers College Record*. www.tcrecord.org/books/Print Content.asp?ContentID=18234.

Hattam, R., & Every, D. (2010). Teaching in fractured classrooms: Refugee education, public culture, community and ethics. *Race Ethnicity and Education*, 13(4), 409–424. doi:10.1080/13613324.2010.488918.

Hope, J. (2008). "One day we had to run": The development of the refugee identity in children's literature and its function in education. *Children's Literature in Education*, 39 (4), 295–304. doi:10.1007/s10583-008-9072-x.

Hope, J. (2011). New insights into family learning for refugees: Bonding, bridging and building transcultural capital. *Literacy*, 45(2), 91–97. doi:10.1111/j.1741-4369.2011.00581.x.

Horlacher, R. (2011). "Best practice" around 1800: Johann Heinrich Pestalozzi's educational enterprise in Switzerland and the establishment of private Pestalozzi schools abroad. *Encounters on Education*, 12, 3–17.

Illeris, K. (2014). Transformative Learning re-defined: As changes in elements of the identity. *International Journal of Lifelong Education*, 33(5), 573–586. doi:10.1080/02601370.2014.917128.

Keddie, A. (2012). Refugee education and justice issues of representation, redistribution and recognition. *Cambridge Journal of Education*, 42(2), 197–212. doi:10.1080/0305764x.2012.676624.

Levitt, R. (2008). Freedom and empowerment: A transformative pedagogy of educational reform. *Educational Studies*, 44(1), 47–61. doi:10.1080/00131940802225085.

Ludke, K., Ferreira, F., & Overy, K. (2014). Singing can facilitate foreign language learning. *Memory & Cognition*, 42(1), 41–52. doi:10.3758/s13421-013-0342-5.

Matthews, J. (2008). Schooling and settlement: Refugee education in Australia. *International Studies in Sociology of Education*, 18(1), 38–45.

Mezirow, J. (1981). A critical theory of adult learning and education. *Adult Education Quarterly*, 32(1), 3–24. doi:10.1177/074171368103200101.

Mezirow, J. (1991). *Transformative Dimensions of Adult Learning*. Jossey-Bass.

Mezirow, J. (1998). On critical reflection. *Adult Education Quarterly*, 48, 185–198.

Mezirow, J. (2003). Transformative learning as discourse. *Journal of Transformative Education*, 1(1), 58–63. doi:10.1177/1541344603252172.

Moreno, S., Lee, Y., Janus, M., & Bialystok, E. (2015). Short-term second language and music training induces lasting functional brain changes in early childhood. *Child Development*, 86(2), 394–406. doi:10.1111/cdev.12297.

Nagda, B., Gurin, P., & Lopez, G. (2003). Transformative pedagogy for democracy and social justice. *Race, Ethnicity and Education*, 6(2), 165–191.

O'Sullivan, E. (1999). *Transformative Learning: Educational Vision for the 21st Century*. Zed.

O'Sullivan, E. (2008). Preface. In M. Gardner & U. Kelly (Eds.), *Narrating Transformative Learning in Education* (pp. ix–xvii). Palgrave Macmillan.

O'Sullivan, E., Morrell, A., & O'Connor, M. (2002). *Expanding the Boundaries of Transformative Learning*. Palgrave.

Onsando, G., & Billett, S. (2014). African students from refugee backgrounds in Australian TAFE institutes: A case for transformative learning goals and processes. *International Journal of Training Research*, 7(2), 80–94. doi:10.5172/ijtr.7.2.80.

Pinson, H., & Arnot, M. (2007). Sociology of education and the wasteland of refugee education research. *British Journal of Sociology of Education*, 28(3), 399–407. doi:10.1080/01425690701253612.

Samway, K., Pease-Alvarez, L., & Alverez, L. (2020). *Supporting Newcomer Students: Advocacy and Instruction for English Learners*. W.W. Norton & Company.

Sellars, M. (2017). *Reflective Practice for Teachers*. Sage.

Sellars, M. (2020). *Educating Students with Refugee and Asylum Seeker Experiences: A Commitment to Humanity*. Verlag Barbara Budrich.

Sellars, M., & Imig, S. (2020). The real cost of neoliberalism for educators and students. *International Journal of Leadership in Education*, 1–13. doi:10.1080/13603124.2020.1823488.

Sonn, C., Grossman, M., & Utomo, A. (2013). Reflections on a participatory research project: Young people of refugee background in an arts-based program. *Journal for Social Action in Counseling and Psychology*, 5(3), 95–110.

Sorgen, A. (2015). Integration through participation: The effects of participating in an English conversation club on refugee and asylum seeker integration. *Applied Linguistics Review*, 6(2), 241–260. doi:10.1515/applirev-2015-0012.

Taylor, E. (2017). Critical reflection and transformative learning: A critical review. *PAACE Journal of Lifelong Learning*, 26, 77–95.

Taylor, S. (2008). Schooling and the settlement of refugee young people in Queensland: '…The challenges are massive'. *Social Alternatives*, 27(3), 58. https://eprints.qut.edu.au/18222/1/18222.pdf.

Wellman, S., & Bey, S. (2015). Refugee children and art teacher training: Promoting language, self-advocacy, and cultural preservation. *Art Education*, 68(6), 36–44. doi:10.1080/00043125.2015.11519346.

Wink, J. (2011). *Critical Pedagogy: Notes from the Real World*. Pearson Education.

# 9    Sharing the leadership challenge

## Introduction

Being a school principal is certainly one of the most important and challenging jobs on the planet. With responsibility for the growth and support of hundreds or thousands of individuals, innumerable daily decisions and rapidly increasing policy and accountability expectations, the role is demanding on a scale that few outside the profession understand. Against the backdrop of these external demands, principals are also tasked with developing and sustaining a school community that is welcoming and supportive of all students. For children and families with refugee and asylum-seeker backgrounds, such a school community is vital for their successful integration into their host country. Developing such a community requires deep reflection, purposeful effort and a willingness to do what is right for each student. This chapter offers research on the effects of the compliance culture in which most leaders operate, the importance of supporting student and staff wellbeing and the power of community to positively transform schools.

## Time to reflect

The multiple roles that school leaders are committed to frequently results in little time for reflection and reflexivity. This essential component of decision-making is often overtaken by the demands of an audit culture which demands not only performance but performativity (Ball, 2003). Performativity, a term introduced by Ball (2003), is not simply about an audit culture and its consequences, but, as Ball (2003, p. 215) writes, is indicative of a much more encompassing manner of governing and regulating those who work in education, most especially school leaders. He states:

> Performativity, it is argued, is a new mode of state regulation which makes it possible to govern in an 'advanced liberal' way. It requires individual practitioners to organize themselves as a response to targets, indicators and evaluations. To set aside personal beliefs and commitments and live an existence of calculation. The new performative worker is a promiscuous

DOI: 10.4324/9781003090731-9

self, an enterprising self, with a passion for excellence. For some, this is an opportunity to make a success of themselves, for others it portends inner conflicts, inauthenticity and resistance. It is also suggested that performativity produces opacity rather than transparency as individuals and organizations take ever greater care in the construction and maintenance of fabrications.

For many leaders who support students with refugee and asylum-seeker backgrounds in their school communities, the comments that Ball makes about 'inner conflicts, inauthenticity and resistance' may be especially salient, most especially on the occasions of decision-making that produce these fabrications of 'opacity' rather than transparency.

Leading schools under departmental and hierarchical regimes which demand that predetermined targets are achieved, or intrusive investigations and interventions are initiated, irrespective of the professional judgements and beliefs of school leaders, is not only a characteristic of an audit culture but a means by which compliance is assured and the need for reflection appears to be minimised (Foucault, 1979; Groundwater-Smith & Mockler, 2009). Despite these impacts of neoliberalised education systems in various parts of the world, in order to remain as responsible, professional leaders, engaging in reflective and reflexive practices remains critical to inform the ways in which these types of targets are interpreted and acted upon in each individual school. Kemmis et al. (2014, p. 10) argue that despite the appearances of performativity, the technical arrangements and sterile discourses of New Public Management practices and neoliberalism in public administration, there are still many individuals engaged in educational endeavours who are not 'dominated' by these constraints. They are everyday school principals, teachers, professional development providers, students and managers who engage daily with the challenges that these deprofessionalising practices invariably inflict upon them. Kemmis et al. (2014, p. 10) state that these individuals 'live their lives in an ordinary practical world luxuriant in critical, moral, economic, social and political and environmental issues – a world that constantly calls forward their best efforts as they rise to meet its challenges.' Though not explicitly referring to school leaders who seek to support students with refugee and asylum-seeker experiences, the individuals of whom Kemmis et al. write reflect the lives and challenges of the principals who participated in the research on which this book is based. Like many other educational leaders in similar contexts and with the multiple challenges of running a school effectively, these participating principals and their teachers, support staff and communities grapple with the ways in which they can, as moral and ethical educational practitioners and civically conscious citizens, meet the particular challenges that their specific contexts and circumstances present as problematic for them. They too do this in the contexts of their everyday work and professional commitments and with thoughtful reflection on the critical aspects of these challenges and their possible solutions. While systems and organisations may engage in relatively anonymous, 'big picture' decision-making and policy design that serve to 'dehumanise' the populations that are the targets of this 'downward gaze' (Ball, 2012, 2016; Gary, 2016; Perryman et al., 2017), school principals are challenged to work in the interpersonal spaces of their own schools and communities and to employ personal and social skills, values and ethical practices to resolve the difficulties presented by these edicts. Contrary to a generally held perception that neoliberalism has de-professionalised education, the participating principals in this research provided proof of the argument presented by Kemmis et al. – these market-driven influences on education have been the catalyst for the development of a new professionalism; a professionalism that is deeply entrenched in a world of people, of collaborative support and, ideally, of shared humane vision for the school and its community.

### Research findings

Each of the principals interviewed for this book expressed a pressing need to know, understand and collaborate with their communities in order to be effective leaders. Two leaders who offered particularly pertinent insights were a primary principal in England and a primary principal in New Zealand.

> Context: We have around 700 children at our school. As our school is improving, our demographics are changing as parents recognise the work we do. We serve a very diverse community. We've got 54 different languages in our school and the community changes all the time.

> *I'm sure there are parents we don't reach out to. But we try: all leadership are outside in the playground in the mornings and we're out there at the end of the day. I'm always out there. It's a chance… I try to stand at different points. I'm not always saying hello to the same parents because the parents who say hello to you, they'll always say hello to you. It's trying to actually observe and think, right, there is a group of parents that are not really engaging or there is a mom over there who is not really talking to anybody. Not in this school, but in a previous school, we had quite a lot of Sri Lankans – when I was outside doing similar duty, I noticed there were quite a lot of Sri Lankan dads and they didn't really engage with the school. They engage with each other. It was lovely to see they formed a little group so they'd obviously all bonded across the playground. They had that common theme.*

> Context: I'm in my thirteenth year of being a principal and this is my third principalship. In total, I've spent 24 years in education. We are one of the most diverse primary schools in the country.

> *One of the real breakthrough moments, sadly, for me as a principal and for many in New Zealand, was after the mosque attacks that happened. We were faced with this new reality all of the sudden, that many of our families had been targeted because of their religion. I never forget the Monday after that, because it happened on the Friday afternoon, and we got in touch with members of the community at the*

*mosque and got some speakers at our whole school assembly to start that week. And from there, the conversations, because we had a cup of tea and something to eat afterwards, with people that I would have just said good morning to and just keep walking. I learned that again, making the time to actually be present with your parents is really significant for them in the learning relationship that then encompasses their child. For a new leader, particularly in a very diverse community, it is important to be visible. Being real is so important as well, and people say all the time being honest with yourself. You really are taken to be that person for your community, because the people that already know how school works, they've already got connections. They've already gotten how it works. What about the others? That may not be the case.*

### Unique contexts, global principles

Each of our leaders see the work of engaging with, listening to, observing and understanding their stakeholders as integral to the success of their schools. Our primary principal from England makes it a priority for her leadership team to be visible and interact with parents before and after each school day. She is purposeful in continually shifting her team members' locations on the playground and she makes it a point to keenly observe parents to identify individuals who may not be connecting with the school community. Her anecdote about the Sri Lankan fathers bonding and the joy she felt captures her concern for ensuring basic human needs of acceptance and belonging. Our New Zealand primary principal shared an anecdote from a very dark time in the country's recent past, following the terrorist attacks in Christchurch's mosques. Though separated by hundreds of kilometres from the violence, her initial response was a deep hurt and sense that her students and families with refugee and asylum-seeker backgrounds were targeted. Connecting with the local mosque provided insight her team didn't possess and helped the school react. Her response to this tragic event strengthened her relationships with many families and affirmed the need to be visible and present. As was the case with our English principal, she stressed the need to learn about and connect with families who don't understand or have not found their place in the community.

Kemmis et al. (2014) assert that the market-driven demands on principals have developed a new type of professionalism, one that is deeply rooted in knowing and fostering community. In a climate dominated by a discourse around academic gains and mounting policy demands, many principals recognise the value of creating a close-knit community of individuals connected to the school and supportive of its mission. Principals must be purposeful in their actions to build and sustain community and vigilant about welcoming those on the periphery. Each of our principals are particularly mindful of the wellbeing and belonging of these individuals and this concern likely diminishes the development of marginalised and discontented stakeholders. Both of our principals work hard to understand their community members and are visible, authentic and engaged and this has developed trust. This trust provides standing to, when needed, push against system policies and expectations they perceive as counter to the needs of their community.

## Building school culture

The ideal of a shared vision for any school is not always easy for principals to achieve, as some of the research participants have noted in their comments. There is no simple pathway to the task of building a school culture that is reflective of the vision and the responsibilities of principals' efforts to integrate students with refugee and asylum-seeker experiences. The complexity of school communities and the interpolated, unique characteristics of each of these, together with the core business of developing learning 'communities of practice' (Lave & Wenger, 1991), has, in the twenty-first century, become increasingly challenging. One significant challenge for many principals has been the market-based influence of the five C characteristics (Competitiveness, Conservatism, Conformity, Conventions and Commerce) of neoliberalist rationalism (Sellars & Imig, 2020), which has changed both the purpose and nature of education. The efficiencies and economies of factory-based practices and standards applied to schooling have served to not only dehumanise what is an essentially interpersonal endeavour (Ball, 2003, 2016) conducted in 'inter-subjective spaces' (Kemmis et al., 2014), but has, in many cases, created a professional and ethical dilemma for school leaders whose vision for school culture is based on care, community and conscience. In many cases, the participants in this research have attempted to push back against this 'downward gaze' (Perryman et al., 2017), with some success. These school leaders have, on occasion, not been as successful as they would have liked to be but persisted in their efforts to support their student cohorts with refugee and asylum-seeker experiences, demonstrating their creativity and commitment by seeking support in other areas of their communities. Much of this approach to successful leadership with regard to integrating these students successfully can be found in Waters et al.'s (2003, p. 2) framework of balanced leadership. They state:

> Our leadership framework is predicated on the notion that effective leadership means more than simply knowing what to do – it's knowing when, how and why to do it. Effective leaders understand how to balance pushing for change while at the same time protecting aspects of culture, values and norms worth protecting. They know which policies, practices, resources, and incentives to align and how to align them with organizational priorities. They know how to gauge the magnitude of change they are calling for and how to tailor their leadership strategies accordingly. Finally, they understand and value the people in the organization. They know when, how and why to create learning environments that support people, connect them with one another, and provide the knowledge, skills and resources they need to succeed. This combination of knowledge and skills is the essence of balanced leadership.

In any modern organisation or system, there are always aspects of structure and governmentality that cannot easily be changed (Foucault, 1991), but developing a shared vision for a specific school is an opportunity for principals to engage with their most critical resource, their teaching and other staff members. The Four Paths leadership model (Leithwood et al., 2017) not only highlights the role of the school leaders in nurturing and supporting their staff personally and professionally; it provides an environment within which to model and contextualise caring and supportive relationships, which in turn impact on the capacities of the staff to share these practices in their interpersonal relationships and to model these for their students. Despite the dehumanising impact of market-driven agendas in schools and curriculum, research findings by Leithwood et al. (2017) strongly indicate that the Emotional Path of the Four Paths model which focuses on leadership skills in teacher wellbeing is highly influential in improving students' academic success. The data provided by the participating principals in this research provided evidence that school culture that focused on affective support as a critical aspect of schooling not only provided students with a sense of belonging and social safety, but it contributed considerably to the potential for academic success.

### Research findings

To a person, each of the principals in our research talked about the importance of developing and maintaining a positive culture for staff, students and all stakeholders. Two leaders who stood out on this topic were a primary principal in the United States and a high school principal in Australia.

> Context: I am the proud principal of my school. Currently, I serve roughly 1,000 pre-kindergarten through 5th-grade students. My school is about nearly 100% free and reduced meals students so we're like a full schoolwide Title 1 program. In addition, I know I'm the most diverse school in the county on the elementary side.

> *We have some amazing teachers at this school. So, the newcomer teachers, they do a lot of home visits with parents, a lot of home visits, a lot of support for parents around how to navigate the school system, how to navigate the city, just all those things. I think we have teachers that do a lot of that work... You know, when I interview people, I always tell them about the school first, like this is what it is, because I think you need a separate set of tools in your toolkit. I realized that a lot of times I'll hire teachers who have had multiple years of experience, but they've never met newcomers or ESOL students. They had a few but like a full school of ESOL newcomers or ESOL students, in general. And I tell them, it's like your first year all over again. But I always tell teachers that we'll have support. Everybody is prepared, I think, in their hearts, and in their minds, like this is going to be a lot of work. When people really realise it's too much, they'll just leave. But for the most part, they stay and they put in the effort and they fall in love with the children. I think that's why a lot of people stay at this school.*

Context: Our school is a relatively small school with around 450 students. We have an 80% EILD background, which means non-English speaking. We also have an Intensive English Centre of about 150 students that comprises refugee international student new arrivals.

*Normally – this is interesting – because we are part of the public education system, we don't have a lot of say in who we hire, necessarily. But if I do have staff coming here, I normally like them to do a sort of trial. They can visit, and it's not whether they have a feeling for the staff, they normally pick up a feeling from the school. There's just a vibe in our school that if you're the right person, you'll want to work here and we have a culturally rich staff as well... For example, I went to a class placement meeting the other day, and it's amazing how well our staff knows each child and their placement and where they need to be. It was a two-hour meeting and staff were so invested, in terms of putting the student or the child in the right place so that they did feel supported, but they also felt challenged because I think that's important. We have temporary staff and non-permanent staff and temporary staff that have been here longer than 10 years and as the principal, I'll do everything I can to try to keep them. I may not be able to give them a permanent position, but I keep employing them because they're part of our family. We talk about the whole word family here.*

### Unique contexts, global principles

Each of our principals were focused on hiring, developing and supporting staff members to support the school vision and maintain a positive school culture. Our principal from the United States is clear with applicants that her school is a more demanding and more challenging environment than other schools and that prior teaching experience will not ensure their success. With her staff, she brings an incredibly developmental approach to her work and makes it clear the school will provide support for success if individuals bring the necessary love and commitment to their work. For teachers unable or unwilling, she supports their departure. Our high school principal from Australia and her team have developed a positive school culture through very hard and rewarding work. While she operates in a system that does not allow her to select her own teachers, she has developed a means of trialling candidates and exposing them to the culture and the work that underpins it, a trial that helps to ensure staff members share the school's vision. Each of our principals have developed a positive culture and focused on hiring staff members who believe in it.

Creating positive culture is the work of every member of a school community. Principals can facilitate this process by hiring staff members who share the school vision or who are open-minded and hard-working enough to come to own the school vision. Once hired, principals must support their staff members personally and professionally. This support, visible to all as relationships and initiatives grounded in care, sets a tone for the entire school community and encourages students, parents, staff and community members to make outreach efforts to others. In such a positive culture, the principal is both a model and a catalyst for improvement as their vision is more likely to be shared and accepted. While caring relationships and a positive culture certainly yield a healthy school environment, effectively working with children and families with refugee and asylum-seeker backgrounds is still a daunting challenge, one that is not for every individual. When efforts to support and develop staff members towards the school's vision fail, leaders must have strategies to move those staff members on to other professions or schools that share their perspective. A school's culture is only as strong as the people who believe in and nurture it and school leaders must remain attuned to this reality.

## Community and conscience

Positive relationships have been recognised for decades as supporting wellbeing, meeting basic human needs and as a means to minimising and healing the impacts of loss and trauma and facilitating improved cognition (De Bellis, 2005; Fredrickson, 2000; Maslow, 1943; Seligman et al., 2005). While the capacity to provide loving care for students traumatised by their refugee and asylum-seeker experiences may be constantly challenged by neoliberalism in its many forms of market-based principles and it impacts on education, the principals who participated in this research provided evidence that pedagogies of love (Darder, 2017; Freire, 1970; Gidley, 2016) and leading with love (Wilkinson & Kaukko, 2020) are the ways in which a real difference can be made to the lives and prospects of these students. While many educators may recoil in horror or amusement at the thought of 'leading with love' or 'pedagogies of love', it is the poverty of the English language that is the catalyst for these reactions. The evidence in the work and words of these school leaders referred to something quite different in nature than the popular notions or romantic love. It referred to a deep commitment to developing community and exercising judgements of conscience.

In developing community, these principals sought to cultivate increasing levels of collaboration between the wider community, among the staff and throughout the student body. Many purposefully sought out pedagogical strategies that had the potential to heal, that gave these students a voice, in addition to providing educational input. They invested in the notion of choice, resisting the common perception that these students and their families needed to assimilate into the majority culture and instead provided learning environments that recognised student and cultural diversity as a school asset; an advantage for the education of non-refugee and asylum-seeker students. In doing this successfully, their schools became a space of emotional and cultural safety and respect, facilitating the development of authentic integration which has the capacity to subtly change the norms and expectations of both cultures (Berry, 1997, 2001; Berry et al., 2006). The development of these communities required commitment to open-mindedness and lack of value judgement regarding the usefulness and validity of different epistemologies and ontologies as a critical aspect of the care and compassion that individuals have the unique capacity to feel for each other and their circumstances. The development of communities such as these raise questions of conscience about the value of all humankind (Mezirow, 1991, 2003) and, indeed, of all life on earth and the husbanding role that has been the responsibility of people since time immemorial (O'Sullivan, 1999; O'Sullivan et al., 2002). In this twenty-first century, critical thinking, criticality and creativity have been nominated among the most important cognitive capacities for students to develop. In the context of communities that offer radical acceptance of difference and diversity, many of the cognitive capacities that comprise these competencies can be developed as discussion, perspective taking, discourse and dialectical process (Sellars et al., 2018).

Preparing refugee and asylum-seeker students for the challenges of living in the twenty-first century is complex and demanding. This is even more so for the school leaders, who, like many of those who participated in the research, find tensions and inconsistencies between their values and beliefs and the institutional demands of their educational policies and systems. It is in these instances that ethical leadership is most valued and most needed. Shapiro and Stefkovich (2016) suggest that, optimally, school leaders should build a personally relevant model of ethical decision-making based on their reflections of formal models of ethical codes, as have many of the principals in this research. The critical aspects of these must include ethics of justice, care and critique, which give meaning to their individual work, their unique contexts and their universal perspectives.

### Research findings

Each of the principals we interviewed made it clear that developing honest relationships with stakeholders is foundational to building a positive school community. Two principals who offered helpful insights were both primary principals in New Zealand.

> Context: Our school has around 500 students and 45 staff members. We have a lot of cultures, but some in very small numbers. I've been a principal here for around 20 years.

> *A welcoming culture is very important to us and has been for a long time. I've had a lot of input on the staff that are here now. I've pretty much employed just about everyone, except for one person. I've had a lot of input and shaping it, so that's something, that all of the staff are people committed to relationships; relationships being fundamental to everything you do. If you don't have a good relationship, it's not a good ground for kids' learning, which is what we're ultimately here for. Everyone needs to know that we see them. We see who they are, we value them, and we want to know them and engage with them. So, the very first step of that as I enrol all students, I meet with all of the parents of the child, we fill in the forms together, and we have conversations and I show them around. So that's the beginning of my relationship with the child, and that's incredibly important.*

Context: I've spent more than 20 years in education and been a principal for more than 10 of those years. I have worked at three schools as a principal. We have around 75 students and 40 staff, with a large number of learning assistants. This school has over 50 nationalities represented.

*So firstly, the aim of our approach is very much based upon the vision of the school, which is focusing on relationships first and making those connections. So, without winning the hearts of families or children, you're not going to create a learning relationship. When I first arrived at this school, it is fair to say that the school was doing a very good job at communicating with the easy to reach families, our European and well-connected families. There was very little home school connection with many of our English-language learners, including refugee families. If you take it back to the version of relationship first, that's what drove our strategic planning. Firstly, our aim became, how are we going to actually reach these families? The second piece that was significantly different for me moving from my first principalship to my second and third – which were far more diverse schools – is "Does your vision and curriculum and charter actually really represent your community, your learners?", because if it doesn't every message that you send home for a newsletter or your website or Facebook page or whatever it is, is just reinforcing again that cultural capital of the people that you already connected with. You're going to always struggle to get the other people on board, unless they can see that they've had a part, no matter how small, and share in your vision of how your school is going.*

### Unique contexts, global principles

Both of our principals spoke extensively about the need to know and develop relationships with their children and families with refugee and asylum-seeker backgrounds. Each leader engages in this relationship building in an unbiased and purposeful manner. Our first primary principal in New Zealand meets with every newly arrived child and family to complete paperwork and to show them around the school. For many families receiving this individualised attention and concern from the principal, an individual seen as having great professional and social status, establishes a strong connection to the school community. This principal also recognises that she is fortunate to have hired her entire staff and each member shares her commitment to building relationships. Our second New Zealand principal is very direct about the need to win the hearts and minds of his families as he believes it is a non-negotiable foundation before learning can occur. To do this, he ensures the school's vision and goals continually reflect the community, particularly as the community's demographics evolve. As a result, the substance, and types, of communications he shares with his community is well received by all. From the moment newly arrived families enrol in their schools, each of these principals are purposeful in their actions to come to know and include them in the community.

Creating places where individuals feel safe, welcome and a sense of belonging is wonderful, purposeful and hard work. Principals who engage in this work, who lead with love, focus on knowing the individuals who comprise the school community and incorporate their beliefs, wants and aspirations into the greater community. While schools operate within a specific regional context and principals are expected to abide by a system's policies, leaders need to recognise that schools are comprised of individuals, many of whom long to be part of a community. Principals must create room within policies to build school communities that reflect all groups, not simply the majority culture. For children and families with refugee and asylum-seeker experiences, principals who care about them as individuals, who know them and who recognise their culture, are vital components of their successful transition to their new lives.

## Chapter conclusion

In this age of hyper-accountability, when schools and school leaders are being held responsible for what ails our societies, resulting policy demands are increasingly tying the hands of school principals. To successfully operate in this environment, leaders must establish positive relationships with students, families, staff and community members. As the educators in this chapter illustrate, relationship building needs to be purposeful, ongoing and shared work for the entire school staff and its benefits are great. Building these relationships around the school's vision and welcoming and involving all stakeholders, including those on the fringe, creates a community vested in the school and the school leader's success. With a vested community, school leaders have the latitude they need to do what is right for every student. In the case of principals serving children and families with refugee and asylum-seeker backgrounds, this latitude is invaluable for pushing against conventions and policies that might otherwise marginalise and impede the journey of students and families in their new home. Through the development of positive relationships, open-minded, caring and reflective leaders truly have the capacity to create spaces of safety and belonging for every child and their families.

## References

Ball, S. (2003). The teacher's soul and the terrors of performativity. *Journal of Education Policy*, 8(2), 215–228.

Ball, S. (2012). *Foucault, Power, and Education*. Taylor & Francis.

Ball, S. (2016). Neoliberal education: Confronting the slouching beast. *Policy Futures in Education*, 14(8), 1046–1059. doi:10.1177/1478210316664259.

Berry, J. (1997). Immigration, acculturation, and adaptation. *Applied Psychology: An International Review*, 46(1), 5–68.

Berry, J. (2001). A psychology of immigration. *Journal of Social Issues*, 7(3), 615–631.

Berry, J. W., Phinney, J., Sam, D., & Vedder, P. (2006). Immigrant youth: Acculturation, identity, and adaptation. *Applied Psychology: An International Review*, 55(3), 303–332.

Darder, A. (2017). *Pedagogies in the Flesh: Case Studies on the Embodiment of Sociocultural Difference in Education* (S. Travis, A. Kearhe, E. Hood, & T. Lewis, Eds.). Palgrave Macmillan.

De Bellis, M. (2005). The psychobiology of neglect. *Child Maltreatment*, 10(2), 150–172. doi:10.1177/1077559505275116.

Foucault, M. (1979). *Discipline and Punish*. Peregrine.

Foucault, M. (1991). Governmentality. In B. Burchell, G. Gordon, & B. Miller (Eds.), *The Foucault Effect: Studies in Governmentality* (pp. 87–104). Chicago University Press.

Fredrickson, B. (2000). Cultivating positive emotions to optimize health and well-being. *Prevention and Treatment*, 3(1), Article 7r. doi:10.1037/1522-3736.3.1.37r.

Freire, P. (1970). *Pedagogy of the Oppressed*. Continuum.

Gary, K. (2016). Neoliberal education for work versus liberal education for leisure. *Studies in Philosophy and Education*, 36(1), 83–94. doi:10.1007/s11217-016-9545-0.

Gidley, J. (2016). *Postformal Education: A Philosophy for Complex Futures*. Springer.

Groundwater-Smith, S., & Mockler, N. (2009). *Teacher Professional Learning in an Age of Compliance: Mind the Gap*. Springer.

Kemmis, S., Wilkinson, J., Edwards-Groves, C., Hardy, I., Grootenberger, P., & Bristol, L. (2014). *Changing Practices, Changing Education*. Springer.

Lave, J., & Wenger, E. (1991). *Situated Learning: Legitimate Peripheral Participation*. Cambridge University Press.

Leithwood, K., Sun, J., & Pollock, K. (2017). *How School Leaders Contribute to Student Success: The Four Paths Framework*. Springer.

Maslow, A. (1943). A theory of human motivation. *Psychological Review*, 50(4), 370–396.

Mezirow, J. (1991). *Transformative Dimensions of Adult Learning*. Jossey-Bass.

Mezirow, J. (2003). Transformative learning as discourse. *Journal of Transformative Education*, 1(1), 58–63. doi:10.1177/1541344603252172.

O'Sullivan, E. (1999). *Transformative Learning: Educational Vision for the 21st Century*. Zed.

O'Sullivan, E., Morrell, A., & O'Connor, M. (2002). *Expanding the Boundaries of Transformative Learning*. Palgrave.

Perryman, J., Ball, S. J., Braun, A., & Maguire, M. (2017). Translating policy: Governmentality and the reflective teacher. *Journal of Education Policy*, 32(6), 745–756. doi:10.1080/02680939.2017.1309072.

Seligman, M., Park, N., & Peterson, C. (2005). Positive psychology progress: Empirical validation of interventions. *American Psychologist*, 60(5), 410–421.

Sellars, M., Fakirmohammad, R., Fischetti, J., Bui, L., Niyozov, S., Reynolds, R., Thapliyal, N., Smith, Y., & Ali, N. (2018). Conversations on critical thinking: Can critical thinking find its way forward as the skill set and mindset of the century? *Education Sciences*, 8(4), 1–29.

Sellars, M., & Imig, S. (2020). The real cost of neoliberalism for educators and students. *International Journal of Leadership in Education*, 1–13. doi:10.1080/13603124.2020.1823488.

Shapiro, J., & Stefkovich, J. (2016). *Ethical Leadership and Decision Making in Education. Applying Theoretical Perspectives to Complex Dilemmas* (4th ed.). Routledge.

Waters, J., Marzano, R., & McNulty, B. (2003). *Balanced Leadership: What 30 Years of Research Tells Us about the Effects of Leadership on Student Achievement*. ASCD.

Wilkinson, J., & Kaukko, M. (2020). Educational leading as pedagogical love: The case for refugee education. *International Journal of Leadership in Education*, 23(1), 70–85. doi:10.1080/13603124.2019.1629492.

# Index

124    *Index*

For Product Safety Concerns and Information please contact our EU
representative  GPSR@taylorandfrancis.com
Taylor & Francis Verlag GmbH, Kaufingerstraße 24, 80331 München, Germany

www.ingramcontent.com/pod-product-compliance
Lightning Source LLC
Chambersburg PA
CBHW070348270326
41926CB00017B/4045